CYBER WARFARE: PREPARING FOR THE NEXT GENERATION OF THREATS

TIRTH PATEL

Made with ♥ on the Notion Press Platform
www.notionpress.com

This book is dedicated to all those who are working to protect us from the ever-growing threats posed by cyber criminals and nation-states. Your hard work and dedication have enabled us to better prepare for the future and better protect ourselves, our organisations, and our networks. This book is a tribute to your efforts and a reminder that cyber security is an ongoing process and a collective responsibility. We thank you for your tireless efforts.

Contents

Foreword

Cyber warfare is a rapidly-evolving field of conflict, and a growing number of countries and organisations are engaging in it. As a result, the threat posed by cybercriminals and nation-states is ever-increasing, and it has become increasingly important to be prepared for the challenges and dangers that lie ahead. This book is a comprehensive guide to understanding and preparing for the next generation of cyber threats. Through an in-depth analysis of the actors, tools, and strategies involved in modern cyber warfare, readers will gain a thorough understanding of the scope and complexity of the challenges posed by cyber warfare. In addition, the book also provides a detailed overview of the ethical, legal, and policy considerations associated with cyber warfare, as well as a comprehensive guide to risk management and mitigation strategies. We hope this book will help readers to better prepare for the future and protect themselves, their organisations, and their networks

Preface

In a world where technology is rapidly evolving and advancing, cybersecurity has become a critical concern for governments, organisations, and individuals alike. Cyber warfare is a complex and rapidly changing landscape, and those who are involved must understand the risks and potential consequences of engaging in it. Cyber threats can come from a wide range of actors, including nation-states, hacktivists, and criminal organisations. This book provides readers with a comprehensive guide to understanding and preparing for the next generation of cyber threats. It includes an in-depth analysis of the actors, tools and strategies involved in modern cyber warfare, as well as an examination of the ethical, legal, and policy considerations associated with cyber warfare. A comprehensive guide to risk management and mitigation strategies is also included, so that readers can be better equipped to protect themselves and their organisations from the growing threat of cyber warfare

Acknowledgements

I would like to express my sincere gratitude to everyone who has contributed to the production of this book. My thanks go to my colleagues and friends who provided invaluable feedback and support throughout the writing process. I am also grateful to the team at my publisher for their invaluable guidance and expertise in helping to make this book a reality. I am also very grateful to the experts who provided their insight and expertise, which has greatly enriched this book. Finally, I would like to thank the dedicated readers of this book, who I hope will benefit from the information and advice provided

Prologue

Cyber warfare is an increasingly prominent concern in today's world. As technology continues to evolve and cyber capabilities continue to expand, the potential for malicious actors to cause disruption and destruction is greater than ever. As the threats posed by cyber warfare become more sophisticated and more widespread, it is essential that individuals, organisations, and governments alike understand the risks and be prepared to respond effectively. This book provides an in-depth look at the actors, strategies, and tools involved in cyber warfare, as well as the ethical, legal, and policy considerations that accompany this new form of warfare. Through a comprehensive exploration of the current state of cyber warfare, this book prepares readers for the next generation of cyber threats.

ONE

Introduction to Cyber Warfare

Introduction:

Cyber warfare is a growing threat that has the potential to cause significant harm to governments, corporations, and individuals. This chapter provides an overview of what cyber warfare is, its brief history, types of cyber warfare, and the significance of cyber warfare in the modern era.

Definition of Cyber Warfare:

Cyber warfare is the use of computer technology to disrupt or destroy the operations of a target organization, government, or military. It is a type of warfare that uses cyber attacks to compromise the confidentiality, integrity, and availability of information systems and networks.

Brief History of Cyber Warfare:

Cyber warfare is not a new phenomenon. The first documented case of cyber warfare occurred in 1982 when the CIA used a Trojan horse program to sabotage a gas pipeline in the Soviet Union. Since then, cyber attacks have become more sophisticated and frequent, with some of the most notable incidents being the Stuxnet worm, the Sony Pictures hack, and the WannaCry ransomware attack.

Types of Cyber Warfare:

There are several types of cyber warfare, including cyber espionage, cyber terrorism, and cybercrime. Cyber espionage involves stealing confidential information from a target organization or government. Cyber terrorism involves using cyber attacks to cause physical harm or disruption. Cybercrime involves using cyber attacks to commit financial crimes or steal personal information.

Significance of Cyber Warfare in the Modern Era:

In the modern era, cyber warfare has become an increasingly significant threat due to the increasing reliance on technology in all aspects of society. The consequences of a successful cyber attack can be devastating, with the potential to cause physical harm, financial loss, and reputational damage. It is therefore important for governments, corporations, and individuals to understand the risks associated with cyber warfare and take measures to mitigate them.

Conclusion:

In conclusion, cyber warfare is a growing threat that has the potential to cause significant harm. This chapter has provided an overview of what cyber warfare is, its brief history, types of cyber warfare, and the significance of cyber warfare in the modern era. It is important for governments, corporations, and individuals to be aware of the risks associated with cyber warfare and take measures to protect themselves against cyber attacks.

Definition of Cyber Warfare:-

Cyber warfare is the use of computer technology and the internet to conduct attacks on the digital infrastructure of a target organization, government, or military. It is a type of warfare that involves using digital weapons to compromise the confidentiality, integrity, and availability of information systems and networks.

In simpler terms, cyber warfare is like a battle fought in cyberspace, where attackers use digital tools and techniques to gain unauthorized access to sensitive information, damage computer systems, and disrupt the operations of a target.

Cyber warfare is a significant threat in the modern era, as virtually every aspect of society is becoming increasingly reliant on technology. Cyber attacks can be launched from anywhere in the world and can cause severe damage to a target's financial, reputational, and operational integrity.

Examples of cyber attacks include phishing, ransomware, denial-of-service (DoS) attacks, and Advanced Persistent Threat (APT) attacks. These attacks are designed to exploit vulnerabilities in a target's computer systems, networks, or applications to gain access to sensitive data, steal intellectual property, or cause disruption.

To defend against cyber warfare, governments, corporations, and individuals must implement robust cybersecurity measures, such as firewalls, intrusion detection and prevention systems, and encryption protocols. They must also develop incident response plans and educate employees and stakeholders about the risks posed by cyber attacks.

In summary, cyber warfare is a growing threat in the modern era that can cause severe damage to individuals, organizations, and governments. It is essential to be aware of the risks associated with cyber attacks and take proactive measures to protect against them.

Brief history of Cyber Warfare:-

Cyber warfare has a long and fascinating history, dating back to the early days of computer technology. In this chapter, we will explore some of the most notable incidents and developments in the field of cyber warfare.

The first documented case of cyber warfare occurred in 1982 when the CIA used a Trojan horse program to sabotage a gas pipeline in the Soviet Union. The program caused the pipeline to malfunction, resulting in a massive explosion. Although the attack was successful, it also highlighted the potential dangers of cyber warfare. In the 1990s, cyber espionage became a significant concern, with governments and intelligence agencies using sophisticated hacking techniques to gain access to sensitive information. The United States and China engaged in a high-profile cyber espionage campaign in the early 2000s, which resulted in the theft of intellectual property, military secrets, and other confidential information. One of the most significant developments in the history of cyber warfare occurred in 2007 when the Russian government launched a cyber attack on Estonia. The attack, which lasted for several weeks, targeted government websites, banks, and other critical infrastructure. The incident marked the first time a nation-state had used cyber warfare to attack another nation's infrastructure.

In 2010, the Stuxnet worm was discovered, which was a highly sophisticated malware program designed to target industrial control systems. The worm was believed to have been developed by the United States and Israel to sabotage Iran's nuclear program.

Since then, cyber attacks have become increasingly frequent and sophisticated, with some of the most notable incidents including the Sony Pictures hack, the WannaCry ransomware attack, and the SolarWinds supply chain attack.

In conclusion, cyber warfare has a rich and complex history, dating back several decades. The evolution of technology and the increasing reliance on digital infrastructure have made cyber attacks an ever-present threat in the modern era. It is important for governments, corporations, and individuals to be aware of the risks associated with cyber warfare and take measures to mitigate them.

Types of Cyber Warfare:-

Cyber warfare involves a range of different tactics and techniques, all of which are designed to disrupt, damage, or destroy the operations of a target organization, government, or military. In this chapter, we will explore some of the most common types of cyber warfare.

Malware attacks: Malware attacks are one of the most common types of cyber warfare. Malware, which is short for malicious software, refers to any program or code that is designed to harm computer systems or steal data. Common types of malware include viruses, worms, Trojans, and ransomware.

Phishing attacks: Phishing attacks are a type of social engineering attack that is designed to trick users into providing sensitive information, such as login credentials or credit card details. Phishing attacks typically involve sending fraudulent emails that appear to come from a trusted source, such as a bank or an e-commerce site.

Denial-of-service (DoS) attacks: DoS attacks are designed to disrupt the operations of a target by flooding its network or website with traffic, rendering it unavailable to users. DoS attacks can be launched from a single computer or from a network of computers that have been compromised by malware.

Advanced Persistent Threat (APT) attacks: APT attacks are highly sophisticated and targeted attacks that are designed to gain access to sensitive information over an extended period of time. APT attacks typically involve a combination of social engineering, malware, and network intrusion techniques.

Insider threats: Insider threats refer to attacks that are carried out by individuals who have authorized access to a target's systems or data. Insider threats can be intentional, such as when an employee steals sensitive information, or unintentional, such as when an employee inadvertently exposes sensitive information.

Supply chain attacks: Supply chain attacks involve targeting third-party vendors or suppliers that are connected to a target organization's network. By compromising a vendor's system, attackers can gain access to the target's network and steal sensitive data.

In conclusion, cyber warfare encompasses a wide range of tactics and techniques, all of which are designed to compromise the confidentiality, integrity, and availability of a target's systems and data. It is important for governments, corporations, and individuals to be aware of these threats and take proactive measures to protect against them. This includes implementing robust cybersecurity measures, educating employees and stakeholders about the risks of cyber attacks, and developing effective incident response plans.

Significance of Cyber Warfare in the Modern Era:

Cyber warfare has become increasingly significant in the modern era, with a growing number of attacks targeting government organizations, corporations, and individuals. In this chapter, we will explore some of the key reasons why cyber warfare has become such an important issue.

Increasing reliance on digital infrastructure: The modern era has seen a significant increase in the use of digital infrastructure, including computer networks, cloud computing, and the internet of things (IoT). This has made it easier for attackers to gain access to sensitive information and disrupt operations.

Globalization: The increasing interconnectedness of the global economy has made it easier for cyber attackers to launch attacks from anywhere in the world. This has made it more difficult for governments and organizations to track down attackers and defend against attacks.

Advanced technology: Advances in technology have made it easier for attackers to develop and deploy sophisticated cyber weapons, including malware, ransomware, and advanced persistent threats (APTs). This has increased the potential damage that can be caused by cyber attacks.

Geopolitical tensions: Cyber warfare has become an important tool for governments to use in geopolitical conflicts. This has led to an increase in state-sponsored attacks and has raised concerns about the potential for cyber warfare to escalate into a full-scale conflict.

Economic espionage: Cyber warfare is often used for economic espionage, with attackers targeting corporations and stealing valuable intellectual property and trade secrets. This can result in significant economic damage and loss of competitive advantage for targeted organizations.

In conclusion, cyber warfare has become an increasingly significant issue in the modern era. The increasing reliance on digital infrastructure, advances in technology, and geopolitical tensions have all contributed to the rise in cyber attacks. It is important for governments, corporations, and individuals to be aware of the risks associated with cyber warfare and take proactive measures to defend against attacks. This includes implementing robust cybersecurity measures, developing effective incident response plans, and engaging in international cooperation to combat cyber threats.

TWO

THE CYBERSECURITY LANDSCAPE

In this chapter, we will explore the current state of the cybersecurity landscape. We will discuss the various threats that organizations face and the challenges they must overcome to defend against them.

The Threat Landscape

The threat landscape for cybersecurity is constantly evolving, with new threats emerging on a regular basis. Some of the most common threats include:

Malware: Malware is a type of software designed to harm or exploit computer systems. This includes viruses, Trojans, and ransomware.

Phishing: Phishing attacks use social engineering techniques to trick people into divulging sensitive information, such as login credentials or financial information.

Denial of Service (DoS): A DoS attack is a type of cyber attack that is designed to disrupt the normal functioning of a website, network or server by overwhelming it with traffic.

Advanced Persistent Threats (APTs): APTs are complex, targeted cyber attacks that are often sponsored by nation-states or other well-funded groups. APTs typically involve a combination of social engineering, malware, and network intrusion techniques.

Insider Threats: Insider threats are attacks perpetrated by people who have authorized access to a company's network or systems. These can be intentional or unintentional.

Supply Chain Attacks: Supply chain attacks involve targeting third-party vendors or suppliers that are connected to a target organization's network. By compromising a vendor's system, attackers can gain access to the target's network and steal sensitive data.

Challenges to Cybersecurity

The cybersecurity landscape is constantly changing and evolving, presenting numerous challenges to organizations trying to protect themselves against cyber threats. Some of the most significant challenges include:

Lack of skilled cybersecurity professionals: There is a significant shortage of skilled cybersecurity professionals, making it difficult for organizations to hire and retain the talent they need to protect against cyber threats.

Complexity of systems: Modern IT systems are incredibly complex, with a multitude of interconnected components. This complexity makes it difficult to identify and address vulnerabilities.

Limited budgets: Many organizations have limited budgets for cybersecurity, which can make it difficult to invest in the technologies and personnel needed to protect against cyber threats.

Inadequate security protocols: Many organizations do not have adequate security protocols in place, leaving them vulnerable to cyber attacks.

Rapidly evolving threats: Cyber threats are constantly evolving, making it difficult for organizations to keep up with the latest threats and technologies needed to defend against them.

In conclusion, the cybersecurity landscape is complex and rapidly evolving, presenting numerous challenges to organizations trying to protect themselves against cyber threats. Organizations must stay vigilant and invest in the technologies, personnel, and protocols needed to protect themselves against these threats. By doing so, they can mitigate the risks associated with cyber attacks and protect their systems, data, and reputation.

Threat actors in the Cybersecurity Landscape:-

Threat actors in the cybersecurity landscape are individuals or groups that use malicious tactics to gain unauthorized access to computer systems or networks. These individuals or groups may be motivated by a variety of factors, including financial gain, political or social motives, or simply a desire to cause chaos or disruption.

One of the most significant threat actors in the cybersecurity landscape is nation-states. These are countries that engage in cyber attacks against other countries for political, economic, or military gain. Nation-states have the resources and technical capabilities to carry out highly sophisticated attacks, and their motivations can range from espionage to sabotage.

Cybercriminals are another significant threat actor in the cybersecurity landscape. These individuals or groups engage in illegal activities online, including theft of personal information, financial fraud, and ransomware attacks. They are motivated by financial gain and may use a variety of techniques to carry out their attacks, including malware, phishing, and social engineering.

Hacktivists are another type of threat actor in the cybersecurity landscape. These individuals or groups use cyber attacks to promote political or social agendas. They may use distributed denial of service (DDoS) attacks or defacement of websites to spread their message and raise awareness of their cause.

Finally, insider threats are a significant threat actor in the cybersecurity landscape. These are individuals who have authorized access to a company's network or systems and use that access to carry out attacks or steal sensitive information. Insider threats may be intentional or unintentional and can be difficult to detect and prevent.

Understanding the motivations and techniques of these different threat actors is crucial for organizations looking to defend against cyber attacks. By implementing strong security protocols, investing in cybersecurity technologies, and staying vigilant for signs of suspicious activity, organizations can better protect themselves against the various threat actors in the cybersecurity landscape.

Common cyber attacks of Cyber Security and Hacking: -

There are numerous cyber attacks that organizations and individuals may face in the cybersecurity landscape. Some of the most common cyber attacks include:

Phishing: Phishing attacks are attempts to obtain sensitive information, such as usernames, passwords, and credit card information, by disguising themselves as trustworthy entities in electronic communication.

Malware: Malware is malicious software that is designed to harm or compromise computer systems. Malware can include viruses, Trojans, worms, and ransomware.

Distributed Denial of Service (DDoS): A DDoS attack is a cyber attack where a website or server is flooded with traffic to make it unavailable to its intended users.

Man-in-the-Middle (MitM): A MitM attack is a cyber attack where the attacker intercepts communication between two parties, giving them access to sensitive information.

SQL Injection: An SQL injection attack is a cyber attack where an attacker injects malicious SQL code into a website's database, allowing them to gain access to sensitive information.

Advanced Persistent Threat (APT): An APT attack is a long-term targeted attack where an attacker gains unauthorized access to a system and remains undetected for an extended period.

Insider Threat: An insider threat is a cyber attack where an individual with authorized access to a company's network or systems uses that access to carry out attacks or steal sensitive information.

These are just a few of the many cyber attacks that organizations and individuals may face. It is important to remain vigilant and aware of the different types of cyber attacks in order to implement effective cybersecurity measures and protect against potential threats.

Vulnerabilities in the Cybersecurity Landscape:-

Vulnerabilities in the cybersecurity landscape refer to weaknesses or flaws in software, hardware, or systems that can be exploited by cyber attackers to gain unauthorized access to data or systems. There are several common vulnerabilities that organizations should be aware of:

Unpatched Software: Unpatched software refers to software that has not been updated with the latest security patches or fixes. Attackers can exploit these vulnerabilities to gain access to a system or data.

Weak Passwords: Weak passwords are easy to guess or crack, and are a common vulnerability that attackers can use to gain access to accounts and systems.

Outdated Operating Systems: Outdated operating systems that are no longer supported by the vendor can be vulnerable to attacks. These systems are often not updated with the latest security patches and are more susceptible to attacks.

Social Engineering: Social engineering is the use of deception to manipulate individuals into revealing sensitive information or taking actions that can lead to a compromise. Attackers can use social engineering techniques to bypass security controls and gain access to systems.

Lack of Security Awareness: A lack of security awareness among employees can also be a vulnerability. Employees who are not trained on proper security practices may inadvertently engage in risky behavior or fall for social engineering attacks.

Default or Weak Configuration Settings: Default or weak configuration settings can also be a vulnerability. Attackers can exploit these settings to gain access to a system or data.

It is important for organizations to regularly assess and identify vulnerabilities in their systems and networks, and to take steps to remediate these vulnerabilities. This may include regular patching and updates, implementing strong password policies, providing security awareness training for employees, and implementing proper configuration settings. By addressing vulnerabilities, organizations can reduce the risk of a cyber attack and better protect their systems and data.

THREE

CYBERSECURITY MEASURES

Effective cybersecurity measures are crucial for protecting organizations and individuals from cyber attacks. There are numerous cybersecurity measures that can be implemented to mitigate the risk of a cyber attack. In this chapter, we will explore some of the most common cybersecurity measures.

Firewalls: Firewalls are a critical security measure that helps protect against unauthorized access to a network. Firewalls monitor and filter incoming and outgoing network traffic based on a set of predefined rules.

Intrusion Detection and Prevention Systems (IDPS): IDPS are systems that detect and prevent unauthorized access to a network or system. These systems monitor network traffic and identify potential security threats.

Antivirus and Antimalware Software: Antivirus and antimalware software are critical for protecting against malicious software. These programs can detect, quarantine, and remove viruses and malware from a system.

Data Encryption: Data encryption is the process of encoding data so that it can only be accessed by authorized users. This helps protect sensitive data from being accessed by unauthorized parties.

Access Control: Access control is the process of controlling who has access to specific resources or systems. This includes implementing strong authentication and authorization policies to ensure that only authorized users can access sensitive information.

Security Training and Awareness: Security training and awareness programs are critical for ensuring that employees are aware of security risks and are equipped with the knowledge and skills to identify and report potential security threats.

Incident Response Plan: An incident response plan is a critical component of an effective cybersecurity strategy. It outlines the steps that should be taken in the event of a security incident, including who should be notified, what actions should be taken, and how to recover from the incident.

Vulnerability Assessments and Penetration Testing: Regular vulnerability assessments and penetration testing can help identify and remediate vulnerabilities in an organization's systems and networks. These assessments should be performed regularly to ensure that vulnerabilities are identified and addressed in a timely manner.

Security Information and Event Management (SIEM): SIEM solutions are designed to monitor and analyze network traffic for security events. These solutions can help detect and respond to security threats in real-time.

Cyber Insurance: Cyber insurance can provide financial protection in the event of a cyber attack. This type of insurance can cover expenses related to data breach notification, legal fees, and other costs associated with a cyber attack.

In conclusion, effective cybersecurity measures are essential for protecting organizations and individuals from cyber attacks. By implementing the cybersecurity measures discussed in this chapter, organizations can significantly reduce the risk of a cyber attack and better protect their systems and data. It is important to regularly assess and update these measures to ensure that they remain effective against evolving threats in the cybersecurity landscape.

-Understanding Cybersecurity Measures:-

Cybersecurity measures are critical for protecting against cyber threats. However, understanding these measures and their effectiveness can be challenging, especially for individuals without a technical background. In this section, we will explore some key concepts to help readers better understand cybersecurity measures.

Defense in Depth: Defense in depth is a cybersecurity strategy that involves implementing multiple layers of security measures to protect against cyber threats. This approach involves implementing measures at different levels, such as the network, application, and user levels. By using multiple layers of security measures, organizations can create a more robust defense system that is more difficult to penetrate.

Risk Management: Risk management is the process of identifying, assessing, and mitigating risks. In the context of cybersecurity, risk management involves identifying potential security threats and vulnerabilities and implementing measures to reduce or eliminate those risks. This can include implementing security measures such as firewalls, antivirus software, and intrusion detection systems, as well as implementing policies and procedures to minimize the risk of a security breach.

Security Controls: Security controls are measures that are implemented to protect against security threats. These can include technical controls such as firewalls and intrusion detection systems, as well as administrative controls such as security policies and procedures. Security controls are essential for ensuring that cybersecurity measures are effective and that security risks are properly managed.

Threat Intelligence: Threat intelligence involves gathering information about potential security threats and vulnerabilities. This information can be used to develop proactive measures to prevent security breaches and to respond quickly to security incidents. Threat intelligence can be obtained through various sources, including security vendors, government agencies, and cybersecurity experts.

Security Audits: Security audits involve assessing an organization's cybersecurity posture to identify potential security risks and vulnerabilities. These audits can be conducted internally or by third-party auditors. The findings of a security audit can be used to identify areas that require improvement and to implement additional security measures.

Cybersecurity Training: Cybersecurity training is critical for ensuring that employees are aware of security risks and are equipped with the knowledge and skills to identify and report potential security threats. Cybersecurity training can include general security awareness training, as well as more specialized training for employees with specific security responsibilities.

In conclusion, understanding cybersecurity measures is critical for protecting against cyber threats. By implementing multiple layers of security measures, implementing risk management practices, and utilizing threat intelligence, organizations can significantly reduce the risk of a security breach. Additionally, regular security audits and cybersecurity training can help ensure that security measures remain effective and that employees are aware of potential security risks.

Types of Cybersecurity Measures:

Cybersecurity measures come in various forms and are designed to protect against a wide range of cyber threats. In this section, we will explore some of the most common types of cybersecurity measures.

Firewalls: Firewalls are a type of cybersecurity measure that acts as a barrier between a computer network and the internet. They are designed to prevent unauthorized access to the network and to block malicious traffic. Firewalls can be hardware-based, software-based, or a combination of both.

Antivirus/Anti-Malware Software: Antivirus and anti-malware software are designed to detect and remove malicious software, such as viruses, worms, and Trojans. They typically use a combination of signature-based and behavior-based detection methods to identify malicious software.

Intrusion Detection and Prevention Systems (IDS/IPS): IDS/IPS systems are designed to monitor network traffic for signs of a security breach. They can detect and prevent attacks such as denial-of-service (DoS) attacks and network intrusions.

Encryption: Encryption is a process of encoding data to protect it from unauthorized access. It is used to protect sensitive data, such as credit card numbers and passwords, during transmission over the internet. Encryption can also be used to protect data stored on computers and mobile devices.

Multi-Factor Authentication (MFA): MFA is a security measure that requires users to provide multiple forms of identification, such as a password and a fingerprint or a one-time code sent to a mobile device. MFA is designed to make it more difficult for attackers to gain unauthorized access to a user's account.

Patch Management: Patch management is the process of regularly updating software and systems to address known security vulnerabilities. It is a critical cybersecurity measure because attackers often target known vulnerabilities in software and systems.

Backup and Recovery: Backup and recovery is a process of regularly backing up data and system configurations to protect against data loss or system failure. It is a critical cybersecurity measure because it can help organizations quickly recover from a security breach or system failure.

Access Control: Access control is a process of limiting access to resources based on user permissions. It is designed to prevent unauthorized access to sensitive data and systems. Access control measures can include password policies, user authentication, and role-based access control.

In conclusion, cybersecurity measures are critical for protecting against cyber threats. Firewalls, antivirus software, IDS/IPS systems, encryption, MFA, patch management, backup and recovery, and access control are just a few examples of the many types of cybersecurity measures that organizations can implement to protect against cyber threats. By implementing multiple layers of security measures and regularly updating and testing them, organizations can significantly reduce the risk of a security breach.

Challenges in implementing Cybersecurity Measures:-

While cybersecurity measures are critical for protecting against cyber threats, implementing them can be a challenging process. In this section, we will explore some of the most common challenges organizations face when implementing cybersecurity measures.

Cost: One of the most significant challenges in implementing cybersecurity measures is the cost. Implementing robust cybersecurity measures can be expensive, and many organizations may struggle to justify the cost. However, the cost of a security breach can be much higher than the cost of implementing cybersecurity measures, making it essential to find a balance between cost and security.

Complexity: Cybersecurity measures can be complex and difficult to implement, particularly for organizations with limited technical expertise. This complexity can lead to mistakes and misconfigurations that can leave an organization vulnerable to cyber threats.

User Education: Cybersecurity measures are only effective if users understand how to use them correctly. Providing user education and training is essential for ensuring that employees understand the risks of cyber threats and how to protect against them.

Compliance: Many industries and organizations are subject to regulatory requirements and standards related to cybersecurity. Compliance with these requirements can be a significant challenge, as they often require a significant investment in time and resources.

Emerging Threats: Cyber threats are constantly evolving, and new threats emerge regularly. Keeping up with these threats and implementing measures to protect against them can be a significant challenge for organizations.

Integration: Cybersecurity measures must be integrated with existing systems and processes, which can be challenging. Failure to integrate cybersecurity measures effectively can lead to gaps in security and leave an organization vulnerable to cyber threats.

In conclusion, implementing cybersecurity measures can be a challenging process. Organizations must consider the cost, complexity, user education, compliance, emerging threats, and integration when implementing cybersecurity measures. By understanding these challenges and working to address them, organizations can implement effective cybersecurity measures that protect against a wide range of cyber threats.

FOUR

Cyber Espionage

Cyber espionage refers to the practice of using digital means to gather sensitive or confidential information from a target, such as governments, organizations, or individuals. It involves the use of sophisticated techniques and tools to penetrate computer systems, networks, and devices to extract data without the knowledge or consent of the owner. Cyber espionage is becoming an increasingly serious concern in the modern world, as more and more information is being digitized and stored on computers and networks. This chapter will explore the various aspects of cyber espionage, including its history, the techniques used, and the impact it has on individuals and organizations.

History of Cyber Espionage

Cyber espionage has been around for as long as computers and networks have been in existence. However, it has only become a major concern in recent years as more and more sensitive information has been digitized and stored on computers and networks. One of the first instances of cyber espionage occurred in the early 1990s when a group of hackers known as the Legion of Doom broke into the computer systems of several major corporations, including IBM and DEC. The group stole valuable information, such as software source code and technical documentation, and sold it to the highest bidder.

Another early example of cyber espionage occurred in 1999 when a group of Chinese hackers broke into the computer systems of the U.S. Department of Defense. The hackers were able to access sensitive information, including missile defense plans and nuclear weapons data. This incident highlighted the potential threat that cyber espionage poses to national security.

Since then, cyber espionage has continued to grow in both frequency and sophistication. Nation-states, such as China, Russia, and North Korea, have been identified as major players in the cyber espionage game. They have used advanced techniques and tools to penetrate the computer systems of other countries, stealing valuable information for their own purposes. In addition, organized criminal groups have also become involved in cyber espionage, using it as a means to steal sensitive information for financial gain.

Techniques Used in Cyber Espionage

Cyber espionage involves a wide range of techniques and tools that are designed to penetrate computer systems and networks, extract data, and cover up any evidence of the intrusion. Some of the most common techniques used in cyber espionage include:

Phishing: This technique involves sending an email or message that appears to be from a legitimate source, such as a bank or company, to trick the recipient into revealing sensitive information, such as login credentials or financial data.

Malware: Malware is software that is designed to infiltrate a computer system and perform malicious actions, such as stealing data or damaging the system. Cyber espionage actors often use malware to gain access to target systems and networks.

Backdoors: Backdoors are hidden access points in a computer system that allow cyber espionage actors to gain entry without detection. Backdoors can be created by hackers who have gained access to a system, or they can be built into software or hardware by the manufacturer.

Social engineering: Social engineering involves the use of psychological manipulation to trick people into revealing sensitive information. Cyber espionage actors may use social engineering techniques, such as posing as a trusted individual or creating a fake identity, to gain access to target systems.

Remote Access Trojans (RATs): RATs are a type of malware that allows cyber espionage actors to remotely control a target computer system. RATs can be used to steal data, install additional malware, or perform other malicious actions.

Zero-day exploits: Zero-day exploits are vulnerabilities in software or hardware that are unknown to the manufacturer or the general public. Cyber espionage actors often use zero-day exploits to gain access to target systems and networks.

Definition of Cyber Espionage:-

Cyber espionage, also known as cyber spying or digital espionage, refers to the practice of using digital means to gather sensitive or confidential information from a target, such as governments, organizations, or individuals. It involves the use of sophisticated techniques and tools to penetrate computer systems, networks, and devices to extract data without the knowledge or consent of the owner.

Cyber espionage is often carried out by state-sponsored actors, such as government agencies or military organizations, but it can also be conducted by criminal organizations or individual hackers. The motivations for cyber espionage can vary widely, ranging from political or economic gain to personal revenge or curiosity.

The types of information targeted by cyber espionage actors can also vary, depending on the goals of the operation. Some common targets include military or government secrets, intellectual property, financial data, and personal information such as social security numbers or medical records.

The methods used to conduct cyber espionage are constantly evolving, as new technologies and vulnerabilities are discovered. Some of the most common techniques include phishing, malware, backdoors, social engineering, remote access Trojans (RATs), zero-day exploits, and advanced persistent threats (APTs).

One of the biggest challenges in combating cyber espionage is the difficulty of identifying and tracking the actors responsible for the attacks. Cyber espionage actors often use sophisticated methods to cover their tracks and make it difficult to trace the origin of the attack.

The impact of cyber espionage can be far-reaching and devastating, both for individuals and organizations. In addition to the loss of sensitive information, cyber espionage can also lead to financial losses, reputational damage, and even physical harm in some cases.

Overall, cyber espionage is a serious and growing threat in the digital age, and it is essential that individuals and organizations take steps to protect themselves against these types of attacks. This includes implementing strong security measures, such as firewalls, antivirus software, and encryption, as well as educating employees and users on how to recognize and avoid potential cyber espionage attempts.

Methods used in Cyber Espionage:-

There are various methods used in cyber espionage, which involve the use of sophisticated tools and techniques to infiltrate computer systems, networks, and devices to gather sensitive information. Here are some of the most common methods used in cyber espionage:

Phishing: Phishing is a social engineering technique used by cyber espionage actors to trick users into revealing sensitive information, such as login credentials or personal data. Phishing attacks typically involve the use of fake emails or websites that mimic legitimate sources to lure victims into providing their information.

Malware: Malware is malicious software designed to infiltrate computer systems and gather sensitive data without the user's knowledge or consent. Cyber espionage actors often use different types of malware, including viruses, trojans, and worms, to infiltrate computer systems and networks.

Backdoors: A backdoor is a secret entry point into a computer system or network that allows cyber espionage actors to bypass security measures and access sensitive data. Cyber espionage actors often create backdoors by exploiting vulnerabilities in software or by using brute force attacks to crack passwords.

Social Engineering: Social engineering involves the use of psychological manipulation to trick users into divulging sensitive information. Cyber espionage actors use a range of social engineering techniques, including pretexting, baiting, and quid pro quo, to gain access to sensitive data.

Remote Access Trojans (RATs): A Remote Access Trojan (RAT) is a type of malware that allows cyber espionage actors to remotely control a computer system and gather data. RATs often go undetected by antivirus software and are difficult to detect and remove once they have infiltrated a computer system.

Zero-Day Exploits: Zero-day exploits are vulnerabilities in software or hardware that are unknown to the manufacturer and have not yet been patched. Cyber espionage actors often use zero-day exploits to gain access to computer systems and networks before the vulnerabilities are discovered and fixed.

Advanced Persistent Threats (APTs): APTs are long-term cyber espionage operations carried out by state-sponsored actors or criminal organizations. APTs involve the use of sophisticated techniques and tools to infiltrate computer systems and networks, often over an extended period of time.

Supply Chain Attacks: Supply chain attacks involve the infiltration of third-party vendors or suppliers to gain access to the target's computer systems and networks. Cyber espionage actors often target smaller vendors or suppliers with weaker security measures to gain access to larger organizations.

Physical Access: Physical access involves gaining access to a target's computer systems and networks by physically entering their premises. Cyber espionage actors may use various tactics, such as posing as maintenance workers or contractors, to gain access to sensitive areas.

In conclusion, cyber espionage actors use a variety of sophisticated tools and techniques to gain access to computer systems and networks and gather sensitive information. To protect against cyber espionage attacks, individuals and organizations need to implement strong security measures and stay vigilant against potential threats. This includes using strong passwords, keeping software up to date, implementing firewalls and antivirus software, and providing regular security training for employees.

Examples of Cyber Espionage:-

Cyber espionage is a widespread phenomenon, and many countries, organizations, and individuals have been targeted by cyber espionage actors. Here are some examples of high-profile cyber espionage incidents:

Operation Aurora: Operation Aurora was a cyber espionage operation conducted by Chinese state-sponsored hackers in 2009. The operation targeted over 30 companies, including Google, Adobe, and Juniper Networks, and resulted in the theft of intellectual property and other sensitive data.

Sony Pictures Hack: In 2014, Sony Pictures was targeted by a group of hackers allegedly linked to North Korea. The hackers stole sensitive data, including unreleased movies, executive emails, and confidential employee information, and caused significant damage to the company's reputation.

SolarWinds Hack: The SolarWinds hack, discovered in December 2020, was a massive cyber espionage operation believed to be carried out by Russian state-sponsored hackers. The attack targeted SolarWinds, a software company that provides network management tools to government agencies and other organizations. The hackers gained access to the company's systems and inserted malware into its software, which was then downloaded by thousands of customers, including government agencies, corporations, and think tanks.

Anthem Data Breach: In 2015, Anthem, one of the largest health insurers in the US, suffered a massive data breach that exposed the personal information of 80 million individuals. The breach was attributed to state-sponsored hackers believed to be linked to China.

Stuxnet: Stuxnet was a highly sophisticated malware program discovered in 2010 that was designed to target Iranian nuclear facilities. The malware was believed to be developed jointly by the US and Israeli intelligence agencies and caused significant damage to Iran's nuclear program.

Operation GhostNet: Operation GhostNet was a cyber espionage operation conducted by Chinese state-sponsored hackers in 2009. The operation targeted over 1,000 computers in 103 countries, including government agencies, embassies, and foreign ministries.

NotPetya: NotPetya was a ransomware attack that targeted several Ukrainian companies in 2017. The attack was attributed to Russian state-sponsored hackers and quickly spread to other countries, causing billions of dollars in damages.

Operation Red October: Operation Red October was a cyber espionage operation discovered in 2012 that targeted government agencies and organizations in over 30 countries. The operation was believed to be carried out by Russian state-sponsored hackers and lasted for over five years.

These examples demonstrate the far-reaching impact of cyber espionage and the significant damage it can cause to individuals, organizations, and even national security. It is essential that individuals and organizations take proactive steps to protect themselves against cyber espionage attacks, including implementing strong security measures, conducting regular security assessments, and staying informed about emerging threats.

FIVE

Cyber Terrorism

Cyber terrorism refers to the use of technology, particularly computer networks and the internet, to carry out terrorist activities. Cyber terrorism is a relatively new and rapidly evolving threat, and it has become a significant concern for governments, law enforcement agencies, and security professionals worldwide. In this chapter, we will explore the definition of cyber terrorism, its characteristics, and the different types of cyber terrorist attacks.

Definition of Cyber Terrorism:

Cyber terrorism can be defined as the use of computer networks and the internet to cause harm or disruption to critical infrastructure, financial systems, or public services with the intention of promoting a political or ideological agenda, creating fear and panic among the population, or achieving some other objective that is consistent with the definition of terrorism.

Characteristics of Cyber Terrorism:

Cyber terrorism is different from traditional terrorism in several ways. Here are some of the characteristics of cyber terrorism:

Global Reach: Unlike traditional terrorism, which is usually confined to a specific geographic location, cyber terrorism can be carried out from anywhere in the world, making it difficult to detect and prevent.

Anonymity: Cyber terrorists can hide their identity and location by using anonymous online tools such as virtual private networks

(VPNs) or the Tor network, making it difficult for law enforcement agencies to track them down.

Low Cost: Cyber terrorism requires relatively little investment compared to traditional terrorism. Cyber terrorists can use free or low-cost tools to launch attacks, making it easier for them to carry out attacks without being detected.

Scale: Cyber terrorism has the potential to cause significant damage on a large scale. A single attack can affect millions of people and cause billions of dollars in damages.

Types of Cyber Terrorist Attacks:

There are several types of cyber terrorist attacks, including:

Distributed Denial of Service (DDoS) Attacks: DDoS attacks are a common form of cyber terrorism. In a DDoS attack, the attacker floods a website or server with a large amount of traffic, causing it to crash or become unavailable.

Malware Attacks: Malware attacks are another common form of cyber terrorism. Malware is software that is designed to damage or disrupt computer systems. Cyber terrorists can use malware to steal sensitive data, disrupt critical infrastructure, or cause other types of damage.

Cyber Espionage: Cyber espionage is the use of technology to steal sensitive information from government agencies, corporations, or other organizations. Cyber terrorists can use cyber espionage to gain access to sensitive information that can be used for political or financial gain.

Cyber Warfare: Cyber warfare is the use of technology to carry out attacks against an enemy's computer systems and networks. Cyber terrorists can use cyber warfare to disrupt critical infrastructure, including power grids, water systems, and transportation networks.

Social Engineering Attacks: Social engineering attacks are a type of cyber attack that involves manipulating people into divulging sensitive information or performing actions that could compromise their security. Cyber terrorists can use social engineering attacks to gain access to sensitive information or to spread malware.

Examples of Cyber Terrorism:

Here are some examples of cyber terrorism:

Stuxnet: Stuxnet was a highly sophisticated malware program discovered in 2010 that was designed to target Iranian nuclear facilities. The malware was believed to be developed jointly by the US and Israeli intelligence agencies and caused significant damage to Iran's nuclear program.

WannaCry: WannaCry was a ransomware attack that affected over 200,000 computers in 150 countries in 2017. The attack was attributed to North Korean state-sponsored hackers and caused billions of dollars in damages.

Ukraine Power Grid Attack: In 2015 and 2016, hackers believed to be linked to Russian state-sponsored hackers carried out a series of attacks on Ukraine's power grid, causing power outages and disrupting critical infrastructure

Definition of Cyber Terrorism:-

Cyber terrorism is a form of terrorism that involves the use of technology, particularly computer networks and the internet, to carry out attacks. The goal of cyber terrorism is to cause harm or disruption to critical infrastructure, financial systems, or public services, with the intention of promoting a political or ideological agenda, creating fear and panic among the population, or achieving some other objective that is consistent with the definition of terrorism.

One of the defining characteristics of cyber terrorism is its global reach. Unlike traditional terrorism, which is usually confined to a specific geographic location, cyber terrorism can be carried out from anywhere in the world, making it difficult to detect and prevent. Cyber terrorists can also remain anonymous by using tools such as virtual private networks (VPNs) or the Tor network, which can hide their identity and location, making it difficult for law enforcement agencies to track them down.

Another characteristic of cyber terrorism is its low cost. Cyber terrorists can use free or low-cost tools to launch attacks, making it easier for them to carry out attacks without being detected. They can also carry out attacks remotely, without the need for physical access to a target's infrastructure.

Cyber terrorism can also have a significant scale. A single attack can affect millions of people and cause billions of dollars in damages. For example, a cyber attack on a power grid could result in a widespread blackout that could affect large regions or even entire countries.

There are several types of cyber terrorist attacks. One of the most common types of cyber terrorist attacks is Distributed Denial of Service (DDoS) attacks. In a DDoS attack, the attacker floods a website or server with a large amount of traffic, causing it to crash or become unavailable. DDoS attacks can be carried out using botnets, which are networks of compromised computers that are controlled by a single attacker.

Another common type of cyber terrorist attack is malware attacks. Malware is software that is designed to damage or disrupt computer systems. Cyber terrorists can use malware to steal sensitive data, disrupt critical infrastructure, or cause other types of damage.

Cyber espionage is another type of cyber terrorist attack. Cyber espionage involves the use of technology to steal sensitive information from government agencies, corporations, or other organizations. Cyber terrorists can use cyber espionage to gain access to sensitive information that can be used for political or financial gain.

Cyber warfare is the use of technology to carry out attacks against an enemy's computer systems and networks. Cyber terrorists can use cyber warfare to disrupt critical infrastructure, including power grids, water systems, and transportation networks.

Social engineering attacks are a type of cyber attack that involves manipulating people into divulging sensitive information or performing actions that could compromise their security. Cyber terrorists can use social engineering attacks to gain access to sensitive information or to spread malware.

In recent years, there have been several examples of cyber terrorism. For example, in 2010, the Stuxnet malware program was discovered, which was designed to target Iranian nuclear facilities. The malware was believed to be developed jointly by the US and Israeli intelligence agencies and caused significant damage to Iran's nuclear program.

In 2017, the WannaCry ransomware attack affected over 200,000 computers in 150 countries. The attack was attributed to North Korean state-sponsored hackers and caused billions of dollars in damages.

In 2015 and 2016, hackers believed to be linked to Russian state-sponsored hackers carried out a series of attacks on Ukraine's power grid, causing power outages and disrupting critical infrastructure.

Types of Cyber Terrorism:-

Cyber terrorism can take various forms and utilize different methods to carry out attacks. In this section, we will discuss some of the most common types of cyber terrorism.

Distributed Denial of Service (DDoS) Attacks

Distributed Denial of Service (DDoS) attacks are one of the most common forms of cyber terrorism. In a DDoS attack, the attacker floods a website or server with a large amount of traffic, making it unavailable to legitimate users. The goal of a DDoS attack is to disrupt the target's services or cause economic damage by making it impossible for customers to access their services or products. DDoS attacks can be carried out by individuals or groups with minimal technical knowledge and can be launched from anywhere in the world.

Malware Attacks

Malware attacks are another common form of cyber terrorism. Malware, short for "malicious software," is any program or code designed to harm a computer system or network. Cyber terrorists can use malware to steal sensitive data, disrupt critical infrastructure, or cause other types of damage. Malware can be delivered via email attachments, infected websites, or other methods. Once installed, malware can take over a computer, steal data, or launch other types of attacks.

Cyber Espionage

Cyber espionage is the use of technology to steal sensitive information from government agencies, corporations, or other organizations. Cyber terrorists can use cyber espionage to gain access to sensitive information that can be used for political or financial gain. The stolen data can be used for blackmail, extortion, or other illegal activities. Cyber espionage attacks are often carried out by nation-states or state-sponsored actors and can be highly sophisticated and difficult to detect.

Social Engineering Attacks

Social engineering attacks are a type of cyber attack that involves manipulating people into divulging sensitive information or performing actions that could compromise their security. Cyber terrorists can use social engineering attacks to gain access to sensitive information or to spread malware. Social engineering attacks can take many forms, including phishing emails, fake websites, and phone calls. Once a victim has been tricked into providing their login credentials or other sensitive information, the attacker can use that information to gain access to sensitive systems or data.

Cyber Warfare

Cyber warfare is the use of technology to carry out attacks against an enemy's computer systems and networks. Cyber terrorists can use cyber warfare to disrupt critical infrastructure, including power grids, water systems, and transportation networks. Cyber warfare attacks can be highly destructive and can cause widespread disruption and chaos. Cyber warfare attacks are often carried out by nation-states or state-sponsored actors and can be used as part of a wider military strategy.

Ransomware Attacks

Ransomware attacks are a form of cyber terrorism that involves infecting a victim's computer with malware that encrypts their files and demands a ransom payment in exchange for the decryption key. Ransomware attacks can be highly profitable for cyber terrorists and have been used to extort money from individuals, businesses, and even governments. Ransomware attacks can cause significant financial and reputational damage and can be difficult to recover from.

In conclusion, cyber terrorism is a serious and growing threat that can take many forms. Cyber terrorists can use a variety of techniques to carry out attacks, from simple DDoS attacks to highly sophisticated cyber espionage and cyber warfare attacks. It is essential for individuals, organizations, and governments to take steps to protect themselves against cyber terrorism and to be prepared to respond quickly and effectively to any attacks that do occur. This includes investing in cybersecurity measures, educating employees and the public about cyber threats, and working together to share information and coordinate responses to cyber attacks.

Case Studies of Cyber Terrorism:-

There have been numerous cases of cyber terrorism in recent years. In this section, we will discuss some of the most notable examples of cyber terrorism and their impact.

Stuxnet

Stuxnet is a computer worm that was discovered in 2010 and is believed to have been developed by the US and Israel as a cyber weapon to disrupt Iran's nuclear program. Stuxnet was designed to target specific industrial control systems used in nuclear facilities and was able to cause physical damage to equipment. Stuxnet is considered one of the most sophisticated cyber weapons ever developed and is a clear example of the potential for cyber terrorism to cause physical damage and disruption.

Sony Pictures Hack

In 2014, Sony Pictures was the target of a cyber attack that resulted in the theft of confidential data, including personal information about employees and unreleased movies. The attack was attributed to North Korea, who was believed to be upset about the upcoming release of the movie "The Interview," which depicted the assassination of North Korean leader Kim Jong-un. The attack resulted in significant financial losses for Sony Pictures and highlighted the potential for cyber terrorism to be used for political purposes.

Ukraine Power Grid Attack

In 2015 and 2016, Ukraine's power grid was targeted by a series of cyber attacks that caused widespread outages. The attacks were believed to be carried out by Russian state-sponsored hackers and demonstrated the potential for cyber terrorism to be used as part of a wider military strategy. The attacks caused significant disruption and highlighted the vulnerability of critical infrastructure to cyber attacks.

WannaCry Ransomware Attack

In 2017, the WannaCry ransomware attack infected hundreds of thousands of computers in more than 150 countries. The attack was believed to have been carried out by North Korean state-sponsored hackers and caused significant disruption to businesses and organizations worldwide. The attack was notable for its use of a vulnerability in Microsoft's Windows operating system, which had been previously discovered by the US National Security Agency (NSA) and later leaked by a group of hackers known as the Shadow Brokers.

Colonial Pipeline Hack

In May 2021, the Colonial Pipeline, which supplies gasoline and other fuels to the eastern United States, was targeted by a cyber attack that resulted in a shutdown of the pipeline. The attack was attributed to a group of hackers known as DarkSide, who used ransomware to encrypt the company's data and demand a ransom payment. The attack resulted in widespread fuel shortages and highlighted the vulnerability of critical infrastructure to cyber attacks.

In conclusion, these case studies demonstrate the real-world impact of cyber terrorism and the potential for cyber attacks to cause physical damage, economic disruption, and even loss of life. It is essential for individuals, organizations, and governments to take steps to protect themselves against cyber terrorism and to be prepared to respond quickly and effectively to any attacks that do occur. This includes investing in cybersecurity measures, educating employees and the public about cyber threats, and working together to share information and coordinate responses to cyber attacks.

SIX

Cyber Warfare and National Security

Cyber warfare has become an increasingly significant threat to national security in recent years. In this chapter, we will discuss the nature of cyber warfare, the potential impact on national security, and the measures that governments can take to defend against cyber attacks.

What is Cyber Warfare?

Cyber warfare refers to the use of technology to conduct offensive and defensive operations in cyberspace. Cyber warfare can involve a range of activities, including espionage, sabotage, and propaganda. It can target government organizations, military facilities, critical infrastructure, and private businesses.

One of the unique aspects of cyber warfare is the ability to conduct attacks from remote locations, making it difficult to attribute responsibility for the attack. Cyber warfare can be conducted by state-sponsored hackers, criminal organizations, or individual actors.

Potential Impact on National Security

The potential impact of cyber warfare on national security cannot be overstated. Cyber attacks can cause significant disruption to critical infrastructure, including power grids, water treatment plants, and transportation systems. They can also compromise sensitive government data, including military secrets and intelligence.

The use of cyber warfare by nation-states has the potential to escalate into a full-blown conflict. For example, a nation-state that has been the victim of a cyber attack may respond with a military attack, which could lead to a broader conflict.

Measures to Defend Against Cyber Attacks

Governments around the world have recognized the threat of cyber warfare and have taken steps to defend against it. These measures include:

Investing in Cybersecurity: Governments are investing significant resources in cybersecurity measures to protect critical infrastructure, government networks, and military facilities. This includes implementing firewalls, intrusion detection systems, and other technologies to detect and prevent cyber attacks.

Developing Offensive Capabilities: Governments are also developing offensive capabilities to respond to cyber attacks. This includes developing the ability to launch cyber attacks against enemy targets, which can serve as a deterrent to cyber attacks.

Building Partnerships: Governments are working together to share information and coordinate responses to cyber attacks. This includes partnerships between government agencies, as well as partnerships between governments and private industry.

Education and Training: Governments are also investing in education and training programs to increase awareness of cyber threats and to provide individuals with the skills needed to defend against cyber attacks.

International Cooperation: Finally, governments are working together to establish international norms and standards for behavior in cyberspace. This includes efforts to prevent the use of cyberspace for malicious purposes, such as cyber warfare and cyber terrorism.

Conclusion

Cyber warfare is a significant threat to national security that requires a coordinated response from governments around the world. While there is no foolproof defense against cyber attacks, governments can take steps to mitigate the risk, including investing in cybersecurity measures, developing offensive capabilities, building partnerships, providing education and training, and establishing international norms and standards. It is essential for governments to remain vigilant and proactive in their efforts to defend against cyber attacks and to adapt their strategies as the threat landscape evolves.

Relationship between Cyber Warfare and National Security

The relationship between cyber warfare and national security is complex and multifaceted. Cyber warfare refers to the use of technology to conduct offensive and defensive operations in cyberspace, while national security refers to the protection of a nation's citizens, territories, and institutions against external and internal threats.

The use of cyber warfare by state-sponsored actors has become an increasingly significant threat to national security in recent years. Cyber attacks can be used to compromise critical infrastructure, steal sensitive government data, and disrupt government operations. This can have a significant impact on a nation's economy, military capabilities, and the safety of its citizens.

One of the unique aspects of cyber warfare is the ability to conduct attacks from remote locations, making it difficult to attribute responsibility for the attack. This makes it easier for state-sponsored actors to conduct cyber attacks without fear of retaliation, further complicating the relationship between cyber warfare and national security.

Governments around the world are investing significant resources in cybersecurity measures to protect critical infrastructure, government networks, and military facilities. This includes implementing firewalls, intrusion detection systems, and other technologies to detect and prevent cyber attacks. However, despite these efforts, the threat of cyber attacks remains high.

Governments are also developing offensive capabilities to respond to cyber attacks. This includes developing the ability to launch cyber attacks against enemy targets, which can serve as a deterrent to cyber attacks. However, the use of offensive cyber capabilities can also lead to a dangerous escalation of tensions between nations.

The relationship between cyber warfare and national security also highlights the importance of international cooperation. Governments are working together to share information and coordinate responses to cyber attacks. This includes partnerships between government agencies, as well as partnerships between governments and private industry. Additionally, governments are working to establish international norms and standards for behavior in cyberspace. This includes efforts to prevent the use of cyberspace for malicious purposes, such as cyber warfare and cyber terrorism.

In addition to state-sponsored actors, cyber attacks can also be conducted by criminal organizations and individual actors. This highlights the importance of educating and training individuals to be aware of cyber threats and to provide them with the skills needed to defend against cyber attacks.

The relationship between cyber warfare and national security is constantly evolving, as new threats emerge and governments develop new strategies to defend against them. It is essential for governments to remain vigilant and proactive in their efforts to defend against cyber attacks and to adapt their strategies as the threat landscape evolves.

In conclusion, the relationship between cyber warfare and national security is complex and multifaceted. Cyber attacks can have a significant impact on a nation's economy, military capabilities, and the safety of its citizens. Governments around the world are investing significant resources in cybersecurity measures to protect critical infrastructure, government networks, and military facilities. However, the threat of cyber attacks remains high, and it is essential for governments to remain vigilant and proactive in their efforts to defend against cyber attacks. International cooperation and the establishment of international norms and standards are critical to ensuring the safety and security of cyberspace.

Examples of Cyber Warfare affecting National Security:-

The use of cyber warfare to attack critical infrastructure, steal sensitive government data, and disrupt government operations has become an increasingly significant threat to national security. Here are some examples of cyber warfare affecting national security:

Stuxnet: Stuxnet is perhaps one of the most well-known examples of cyber warfare affecting national security. The malware was designed to target Iran's nuclear facilities and disrupt their uranium enrichment program. It is believed that Stuxnet was developed by the United States and Israel, and it caused significant damage to Iran's nuclear program.

Russian interference in the 2016 U.S. Presidential Election: Russian operatives used a combination of social media manipulation, hacking, and leaks to interfere in the 2016 U.S. Presidential election. The interference was aimed at influencing the outcome of the election and causing political chaos in the United States. The incident highlighted the vulnerability of the U.S. electoral system to cyber attacks and the potential impact of such attacks on national security.

NotPetya: NotPetya is a type of ransomware that was used in a cyber attack on Ukraine in 2017. The attack targeted critical infrastructure, including government agencies, power plants, and airports. The attack caused significant disruption to the country's infrastructure and highlighted the potential for cyber attacks to cause physical damage and disruption.

Chinese hacking of U.S. government data: In 2015, Chinese hackers breached the Office of Personnel Management (OPM) and stole sensitive data on millions of U.S. government employees. The breach was believed to be part of a larger Chinese espionage campaign aimed at stealing U.S. government data. The incident highlighted the vulnerability of government networks to cyber attacks and the potential impact of such attacks on national security.

Cyber attacks on the Ukrainian power grid: Ukraine has been the target of several cyber attacks on its power grid. In 2015, a cyber attack caused a power outage in parts of the country, leaving hundreds of thousands of people without electricity. The attack was attributed to Russian hackers and highlighted the potential for cyber attacks to cause physical damage and disruption to critical infrastructure.

Iranian hacking of U.S. military systems: In 2013, Iranian hackers breached a U.S. Navy computer system and stole sensitive data on naval operations. The incident highlighted the vulnerability of military networks to cyber attacks and the potential impact of such attacks on national security.

These examples demonstrate the significant impact that cyber warfare can have on national security. Cyber attacks can be used to compromise critical infrastructure, steal sensitive government data, and disrupt government operations. They can also cause physical damage and disruption, as demonstrated by the cyber attacks on the Ukrainian power grid. It is essential for governments to remain vigilant and proactive in their efforts to defend against cyber attacks and to adapt their strategies as the threat landscape evolves.

The need for a National Cybersecurity Strategy

As cyber threats continue to evolve and become more sophisticated, the need for a National Cybersecurity Strategy has become increasingly important. A comprehensive national cybersecurity strategy can help protect critical infrastructure, secure government and private sector networks, and ensure the safety and security of citizens.

Here are some of the reasons why a National Cybersecurity Strategy is needed:

Protecting Critical Infrastructure: Critical infrastructure refers to the systems and assets that are vital to the functioning of society, such as power grids, water treatment plants, and transportation systems. These systems are increasingly connected to the internet, making them vulnerable to cyber attacks. A National Cybersecurity Strategy can help protect critical infrastructure by establishing cybersecurity standards and best practices, promoting information sharing between government and private sector stakeholders, and investing in cybersecurity research and development.

Securing Government Networks: Governments are responsible for a vast amount of sensitive information, including classified information, personal information, and financial information. Government networks are also critical to the functioning of government operations. A National Cybersecurity Strategy can help secure government networks by establishing cybersecurity standards and best practices, implementing risk management strategies, and investing in cybersecurity training and awareness programs.

Protecting Private Sector Networks: Private sector networks are also vulnerable to cyber attacks, and the consequences of a successful attack can be significant, both for the company and for the economy as a whole. A National Cybersecurity Strategy can help protect private sector networks by promoting cybersecurity standards and best practices, encouraging information sharing between government and private sector stakeholders, and incentivizing investment in cybersecurity.

Ensuring the Safety and Security of Citizens: Cybersecurity is not just about protecting networks and systems; it is also about protecting people. Cyber attacks can lead to the theft of personal information, financial fraud, and other forms of criminal activity. A National Cybersecurity Strategy can help ensure the safety and security of citizens by promoting cybersecurity awareness and education, encouraging the development of secure technologies, and investing in law enforcement and other resources to combat cyber crime.

Addressing International Cyber Threats: Cyber threats are not limited to national borders; they are global in nature. A National Cybersecurity Strategy can help address international cyber threats by promoting international cooperation and collaboration, establishing international cybersecurity standards, and working with international partners to combat cyber crime and other cyber threats.

In summary, a National Cybersecurity Strategy is essential for protecting critical infrastructure, securing government and private sector networks, ensuring the safety and security of citizens, and addressing international cyber threats. Governments must work together to develop comprehensive cybersecurity strategies that prioritize cybersecurity education, awareness, and investment in research and development. By taking a proactive approach to cybersecurity, governments can help ensure that the benefits of technology are realized while minimizing the risks.

SEVEN
Legal Frameworks for Cyber Warfare

Introduction:

Cyber warfare has become an increasingly significant issue in modern-day warfare due to the development and advancement of technology. Countries have developed sophisticated cyber weapons that can be used to launch attacks against other countries, which can cause significant damage to critical infrastructure and result in loss of life. Legal frameworks for cyber warfare are necessary to ensure that cyber operations are conducted in accordance with international law. This chapter will discuss the legal frameworks for cyber warfare, including international law, domestic law, and military law.

International Law:

International law is a set of rules and principles that govern the relations between states. It is composed of treaties, conventions, and customary international law. The primary framework for international law is the United Nations Charter, which sets out the fundamental principles of international law. The Charter prohibits the use of force in international relations, with the exception of self-defense and collective defense.

The use of force in cyberspace is a controversial issue because it is difficult to determine the source of an attack and the extent of damage caused. However, international law applies to cyberspace, and countries are bound by their obligations under international law. The Tallinn Manual 2.0 is a comprehensive guide to the international law applicable to cyber operations. It sets out the legal framework for cyber operations and provides guidance on the legal implications of cyber operations.

Domestic Law:

Domestic law is the law of a particular country. Each country has its own legal framework for cyber operations. Domestic law regulates the conduct of cyber operations by government agencies and private entities. The legal framework for cyber operations varies from country to country, but it typically includes laws that criminalize unauthorized access to computer systems, data theft, and other cyber crimes.

In the United States, the primary law governing cyber operations is the Computer Fraud and Abuse Act (CFAA). The CFAA criminalizes unauthorized access to computer systems and data theft. The law has been used to prosecute hackers and other cyber criminals. The United Kingdom has similar laws, including the Computer Misuse Act, which criminalizes unauthorized access to computer systems.

Military Law:

Military law is the law that governs the conduct of military operations. The law includes rules on the use of force, the treatment of prisoners of war, and the protection of civilians. Military law also applies to cyber operations conducted by the military. The military has its own legal framework for cyber operations, which includes rules of engagement, operational law, and military doctrine.

The United States has established a comprehensive legal framework for cyber operations. The Department of Defense has issued several directives and policies that govern the conduct of cyber operations. These include the Department of Defense

Directive 8570.01, which establishes the requirements for information assurance workforce certification, and the Joint Publication 3-12, which provides guidance on the planning and execution of cyber operations.

Conclusion:

Legal frameworks for cyber warfare are necessary to ensure that cyber operations are conducted in accordance with international law. International law, domestic law, and military law provide the legal framework for cyber operations. The legal framework for cyber operations varies from country to country, but it typically includes laws that criminalize unauthorized access to computer systems, data theft, and other cyber crimes. The development of a comprehensive legal framework for cyber warfare is essential to protect critical infrastructure and ensure the safety of civilians.

International legal frameworks for Cyber Warfare

Introduction:

The development of cyber warfare has created a new challenge for international law. The use of cyber weapons can cause significant damage to critical infrastructure and result in loss of life. International law provides the legal framework for cyber warfare and sets out the rules and principles that govern the relations between states. This chapter will discuss the international legal frameworks for cyber warfare, including the United Nations Charter, the International Covenant on Civil and Political Rights (ICCPR), and the Tallinn Manual 2.0.

The United Nations Charter:

The United Nations Charter is the primary framework for international law. It sets out the fundamental principles of international law, including the prohibition of the use of force in international relations. The Charter allows for the use of force in self-defense and collective defense. However, the use of force in cyberspace is a controversial issue because it is difficult to determine the source of an attack and the extent of damage caused.

The International Covenant on Civil and Political Rights:

The International Covenant on Civil and Political Rights (ICCPR) is a multilateral treaty that sets out the basic rights and freedoms of individuals. The treaty was adopted by the United Nations General Assembly in 1966 and has been ratified by 173 countries. The ICCPR is one of the most important international legal frameworks for cyber warfare because it sets out the fundamental rights that must be protected in cyberspace.

The ICCPR recognizes the right to privacy, the right to freedom of expression, and the right to freedom of association. These rights are essential for the protection of individuals in cyberspace. The ICCPR also requires states to take measures to protect the rights of individuals from interference by third parties. This includes the protection of individuals from cyber attacks.

The Tallinn Manual 2.0:

The Tallinn Manual 2.0 is a comprehensive guide to the international law applicable to cyber operations. It was produced by a group of legal experts and is widely recognized as the most authoritative source of guidance on the legal implications of cyber operations. The manual sets out the legal framework for cyber operations and provides guidance on how international law applies to cyberspace.

The manual covers a range of topics, including the use of force in cyberspace, the attribution of cyber attacks, and the protection of critical infrastructure. It also provides guidance on the rules of engagement for cyber operations, the use of cyber weapons, and the protection of civilians.

Conclusion:

International legal frameworks for cyber warfare are essential to ensure that cyber operations are conducted in accordance with international law. The United Nations Charter, the International Covenant on Civil and Political Rights, and the Tallinn Manual 2.0 provide the legal framework for cyber operations. These legal frameworks set out the rules and principles that govern the relations between states and provide guidance on how international law applies to cyberspace. The development of a comprehensive legal framework for cyber warfare is essential to protect critical infrastructure and ensure the safety of civilians.

Ethical considerations in Cyber Warfare:-

Ethics plays a crucial role in all aspects of warfare, including cyber warfare. The use of cyber weapons can cause significant damage to critical infrastructure and result in loss of life. Cyber warfare raises many ethical questions, including the justifiability of using cyber weapons, the attribution of cyber attacks, and the protection of civilians. This chapter will discuss the ethical considerations in cyber warfare and provide insights into how states should approach these issues.

Just War Theory:

Just War Theory provides a framework for assessing the morality of using force in international relations. The theory sets out two categories of criteria: jus ad bellum (the right to go to war) and jus in bello (the right conduct of war). Applying these criteria to cyber warfare raises several ethical questions.

Firstly, the jus ad bellum criteria require states to have a just cause, to have exhausted all other options, and to have a reasonable chance of success. In cyber warfare, it is challenging to determine if these criteria are met. The source of a cyber attack may be difficult to attribute, and it may be unclear if other options were considered.

Secondly, the jus in bello criteria require states to use proportional force, avoid targeting civilians, and respect the principle of distinction. In cyber warfare, it is challenging to determine the proportionality of a cyber attack, and the principle of distinction can be difficult to apply.

Attribution:

Attribution is a significant challenge in cyber warfare. Cyber attacks can be launched from anywhere in the world and may be difficult to trace. The difficulty of attribution raises ethical questions about the justifiability of using force in response to a cyber attack.

The difficulty of attribution also raises questions about the accuracy of intelligence. If a state responds to a cyber attack based on faulty intelligence, it may cause significant harm to innocent civilians.

Protection of Civilians:

The protection of civilians is a fundamental principle of international humanitarian law. In cyber warfare, civilians are vulnerable to the effects of cyber attacks, including disruption of critical infrastructure and loss of personal data.

States have a responsibility to take all feasible precautions to protect civilians from harm. This includes ensuring that critical infrastructure is secure and that civilians are informed of the risks of cyber attacks.

Cyber Security and Cyber Defense:

Ethical considerations in cyber warfare also extend to cyber security and cyber defense. States have a responsibility to ensure that their cyber security measures do not harm innocent civilians or violate their rights.

Cyber defense measures must also respect the principle of proportionality. The use of defensive measures that cause significant harm to the attacker may be considered disproportionate.

EIGHT

Cyber Intelligence

Introduction:

Cyber intelligence is a critical component of cybersecurity, providing organizations with the information necessary to identify, prevent, and respond to cyber threats. Cyber intelligence involves collecting, analyzing, and disseminating information about potential cyber threats, as well as identifying vulnerabilities in information systems. This chapter will discuss the various aspects of cyber intelligence, including collection methods, analysis techniques, and the role of cyber intelligence in cybersecurity operations.

Collection Methods:

Cyber intelligence collection methods can be divided into two main categories: passive and active. Passive collection methods involve monitoring network traffic, analyzing open-source information, and conducting social media analysis. Active collection methods involve engaging with potential threats, such as conducting reconnaissance on threat actors and infiltrating their networks.

Passive collection methods are less intrusive and can provide valuable information about potential threats. However, they are limited by the amount of information available and may not be able to identify more sophisticated threats. Active collection methods, while more intrusive, can provide more detailed information about potential threats, but also carry greater risks.

Analysis Techniques:

Cyber intelligence analysis involves processing and interpreting information collected from various sources. Analysis techniques can be divided into two main categories: human analysis and machine analysis.

Human analysis involves the use of trained analysts to process and interpret information. Human analysis can provide a more nuanced understanding of potential threats and can identify patterns that may not be immediately apparent. However, human analysis is time-consuming and can be subject to bias.

Machine analysis involves the use of artificial intelligence (AI) and machine learning algorithms to process and interpret information. Machine analysis can process large amounts of data quickly and can identify patterns that may be missed by human analysts. However, machine analysis is limited by the quality of the data and the accuracy of the algorithms.

Role in Cybersecurity Operations:

Cyber intelligence plays a critical role in cybersecurity operations, providing organizations with the information necessary to identify and prevent potential cyber threats. Cyber intelligence is used to identify vulnerabilities in information systems, monitor network activity, and detect potential threats.

Cyber intelligence is also used to support incident response and remediation efforts. In the event of a cyber attack, cyber intelligence can be used to identify the source of the attack and provide information necessary for incident response and remediation efforts.

Challenges:

Cyber intelligence faces several challenges, including the difficulty of collecting and analyzing large amounts of data, the complexity of the threat landscape, and the rapidly evolving nature of cyber threats. Additionally, cyber intelligence is subject to bias, both in the collection and analysis phases.

Another challenge in cyber intelligence is the need for effective information sharing. Information sharing between organizations can help to identify potential threats and vulnerabilities, but there are significant barriers to effective information sharing, including legal and organizational constraints.

Conclusion:

Cyber intelligence is a critical component of cybersecurity, providing organizations with the information necessary to identify, prevent, and respond to cyber threats. Cyber intelligence collection methods can be passive or active, and analysis techniques can be human or machine-based. Cyber intelligence plays a vital role in cybersecurity operations, identifying vulnerabilities, monitoring network activity, and supporting incident response and remediation efforts. However, cyber intelligence faces several challenges, including the complexity of the threat landscape and the need for effective information sharing.

Definition of Cyber Intelligence:-

Cyber Intelligence is a field that is rapidly evolving due to the constantly changing nature of cyber threats and attacks. As such, the definition of Cyber Intelligence can vary depending on the context in which it is used. However, at its core, Cyber Intelligence refers to the collection, analysis, and dissemination of information related to potential or actual cyber threats and vulnerabilities.

Cyber Intelligence is a critical component of cybersecurity, as it provides valuable insights into the tactics, techniques, and procedures (TTPs) used by threat actors to infiltrate and compromise systems. This information is used by organizations to proactively defend against cyber attacks and to respond quickly and effectively when they occur.

The collection of Cyber Intelligence involves the use of various techniques, tools, and technologies to gather information from different sources. These sources may include open-source intelligence (OSINT), social media, dark web forums, and other online communities where threat actors may congregate.

The analysis of Cyber Intelligence involves the use of data analytics and other techniques to identify patterns and trends in the information collected. This analysis is used to identify potential threats, assess their likelihood and severity, and develop appropriate mitigation strategies.

The dissemination of Cyber Intelligence involves sharing the insights and findings with relevant stakeholders. This may include security teams within an organization, law enforcement agencies, government agencies, and other organizations that may be at risk of cyber attacks.

Cyber Intelligence is also used to support other areas of cybersecurity, such as incident response, threat hunting, and vulnerability management. By leveraging the insights provided by Cyber Intelligence, organizations can better understand the threat landscape and take proactive steps to protect themselves from potential attacks.

One of the key challenges of Cyber Intelligence is keeping up with the constantly evolving threat landscape. Threat actors are constantly developing new tactics and techniques to evade detection, and as such, Cyber Intelligence must be constantly updated to stay relevant.

In addition to the technical aspects of Cyber Intelligence, there are also legal and ethical considerations to be aware of. The collection and analysis of Cyber Intelligence must be done in compliance with relevant laws and regulations, and organizations must also be aware of the potential privacy implications of collecting and analyzing data.

In conclusion, Cyber Intelligence is a critical component of modern cybersecurity. By collecting, analyzing, and disseminating information related to potential or actual cyber threats, organizations can better understand the threat landscape and take proactive steps to protect themselves from potential attacks. However, it is important to keep in mind the constantly evolving nature of cyber threats and the legal and ethical considerations that must be taken into account when collecting and analyzing Cyber Intelligence.

Methods used in Cyber Intelligence:-

Cyber intelligence is the process of collecting, analyzing, and disseminating information related to potential cyber threats. In order to gather and analyze cyber intelligence, a wide range of methods and techniques are employed. This chapter will discuss the various methods used in cyber intelligence, including open source intelligence, human intelligence, signals intelligence, and technical intelligence.

Open Source Intelligence (OSINT):

Open source intelligence involves collecting and analyzing information from publicly available sources. This can include information from websites, social media platforms, news articles, and other sources. OSINT can provide valuable information about potential cyber threats, including information about the tactics, techniques, and procedures (TTPs) used by threat actors.

Human Intelligence (HUMINT):

Human intelligence involves collecting information through direct engagement with individuals or groups. This can involve interviewing individuals, conducting surveys, or engaging in other forms of direct communication. HUMINT can provide valuable insights into potential cyber threats, including information about the motivations and intentions of threat actors.

Signals Intelligence (SIGINT):

Signals intelligence involves collecting and analyzing information from communication systems. This can include intercepting and decoding communications between threat actors, as well as analyzing network traffic to identify potential threats. SIGINT can provide valuable information about the capabilities and intentions of potential threat actors.

Technical Intelligence (TECHINT):

Technical intelligence involves collecting and analyzing information related to technical systems and infrastructure. This can include analyzing vulnerabilities in software systems, reverse engineering malware, and identifying potential attack vectors. TECHINT can provide valuable insights into potential cyber threats, including information about the tools and techniques used by threat actors.

Open-Source Intelligence Tools and Techniques:

There are various tools and techniques used in OSINT collection and analysis. Some of these include search engines, social media monitoring tools, and web scraping tools. These tools can be used to collect and analyze data from a variety of sources, including social media platforms, news articles, and other online sources.

Human Intelligence Techniques:

HUMINT techniques can include conducting interviews with individuals who have knowledge of potential cyber threats, developing relationships with insiders who can provide valuable information, and conducting surveys or polls to gather information about potential threats. HUMINT can provide valuable insights into the motivations and intentions of threat actors, as well as their capabilities and resources.

Signals Intelligence Techniques:

SIGINT techniques can include intercepting and analyzing communication signals, including radio, satellite, and cellular signals. This can involve the use of sophisticated equipment to collect and analyze data, as well as the use of advanced software tools to decode and interpret data.

Technical Intelligence Techniques:

TECHINT techniques can include analyzing software code and network traffic, reverse engineering malware, and identifying vulnerabilities in software systems. This can involve the use of specialized software tools and techniques, as well as the expertise of highly skilled technical analysts.

Conclusion:

Cyber intelligence is a critical component of cybersecurity, providing organizations with the information necessary to identify and prevent potential cyber threats. There are various methods and techniques used in cyber intelligence, including open source intelligence, human intelligence, signals intelligence, and technical intelligence. Each of these methods provides valuable insights into potential cyber threats and can be used in conjunction with one another to provide a more comprehensive understanding of the threat landscape. The use of specialized tools and techniques can also help to improve the effectiveness of cyber intelligence collection and analysis.

Examples of Cyber Intelligence:-

Cyber Intelligence is a broad field that encompasses a wide range of activities and techniques. Here are some examples of Cyber Intelligence:

Threat intelligence: Threat intelligence involves the collection, analysis, and dissemination of information related to potential or actual cyber threats. This may include information on known threat actors, their tactics, techniques, and procedures (TTPs), and the tools and malware they use. Threat intelligence is used to identify potential threats and develop appropriate mitigation strategies.

Vulnerability intelligence: Vulnerability intelligence involves the collection, analysis, and dissemination of information related to software and hardware vulnerabilities. This information is used to identify vulnerabilities that could be exploited by threat actors and develop appropriate mitigation strategies.

Social media intelligence: Social media intelligence involves the collection, analysis, and dissemination of information from social media platforms. This information can be used to identify potential threats, monitor brand reputation, and gather information on competitors.

Dark web intelligence: Dark web intelligence involves the collection, analysis, and dissemination of information from dark web forums and marketplaces. This information can be used to identify potential threats, monitor the sale of stolen data, and gather intelligence on threat actors.

Incident response: Incident response involves the collection, analysis, and dissemination of information related to a cyber incident. This may include forensic analysis of compromised systems, network traffic analysis, and analysis of malware used in the attack.

Threat hunting: Threat hunting involves proactively searching for potential threats that may have evaded detection by traditional security measures. This may involve analyzing logs, network traffic, and other data sources to identify anomalous behavior that may be indicative of a potential threat.

Cybercrime investigations: Cybercrime investigations involve the collection, analysis, and dissemination of information related to criminal activity in the cyber realm. This may include investigations into hacking, malware distribution, identity theft, and other cybercrimes.

Cybersecurity risk assessments: Cybersecurity risk assessments involve the collection, analysis, and dissemination of information related to an organization's cybersecurity risks. This may include assessing vulnerabilities in systems and networks, evaluating the effectiveness of existing security controls, and identifying areas where additional controls may be necessary.

Cybersecurity threat assessments: Cybersecurity threat assessments involve the collection, analysis, and dissemination of information related to the threat landscape facing an organization. This may include evaluating the capabilities and motivations of threat actors, identifying emerging threats, and assessing the likelihood and potential impact of potential cyber attacks.

These are just a few examples of the many different types of Cyber Intelligence activities that can be undertaken. By collecting, analyzing, and disseminating information related to potential or actual cyber threats, organizations can better understand the threat landscape and take proactive steps to protect themselves from potential attacks.

NINE

CYBER WARFARE AND CORPORATE SECURITY

Introduction:

As cyber threats continue to increase in frequency and sophistication, it is essential for corporations to develop robust cybersecurity strategies to protect their assets and sensitive information. This chapter will explore the relationship between cyber warfare and corporate security, examining the ways in which corporations can mitigate the risks of cyber attacks and respond effectively to incidents when they occur.

The Nature of Cyber Warfare:

Cyber warfare involves the use of technology to disrupt, damage, or destroy computer systems, networks, or infrastructure. Cyber attacks can be carried out by a range of threat actors, including nation-states, criminal organizations, and individual hackers. The consequences of cyber attacks can be severe, resulting in the loss of sensitive information, disruption of critical systems, and significant financial losses.

Corporate Security in the Face of Cyber Threats:

Given the increasing threat of cyber attacks, corporations must develop comprehensive cybersecurity strategies to protect their assets and sensitive information. Some key components of an effective cybersecurity strategy include:

Risk assessment: Conducting a thorough assessment of the risks facing the organization, including identifying potential threat actors and vulnerabilities in systems and infrastructure.

Access control: Limiting access to sensitive information and critical systems to authorized personnel only.

Monitoring and detection: Implementing systems and processes to detect and respond to potential cyber threats in real-time.

Incident response: Developing a robust incident response plan to minimize the impact of cyber attacks and ensure business continuity.

Employee training: Providing regular training to employees on cybersecurity best practices and potential threats.

Cybersecurity Best Practices for Corporations:

In addition to the key components of an effective cybersecurity strategy outlined above, there are a number of best practices that corporations can adopt to enhance their cybersecurity posture. These include:

Encryption: Implementing encryption technologies to protect sensitive data both in transit and at rest.

Multi-factor authentication: Implementing multi-factor authentication to reduce the risk of unauthorized access to critical systems and information.

Regular software updates and patches: Ensuring that all software and systems are regularly updated with the latest security patches and updates.

Third-party risk management: Conducting due diligence on third-party vendors and suppliers to ensure that they have adequate cybersecurity measures in place.

Regular cybersecurity assessments: Conducting regular assessments of cybersecurity practices and systems to identify and address potential vulnerabilities.

Conclusion:

The threat of cyber attacks is a serious concern for corporations in all industries, and the consequences of a successful attack can be severe. To mitigate the risks of cyber attacks and protect their assets and sensitive information, corporations must develop comprehensive cybersecurity strategies that include risk assessment, access control, monitoring and detection, incident response, and employee training. Adopting cybersecurity best practices, such as encryption, multi-factor authentication, and regular software updates and patches, can further enhance a corporation's cybersecurity posture. By taking these steps, corporations can better protect themselves against the increasing threat of cyber warfare.

Relationship between Cyber Warfare and Corporate Security

Cyber Warfare and Corporate Security are two distinct areas, but they are closely related in the context of modern cybersecurity. Cyber Warfare refers to the use of cyber capabilities by nation-states or other actors to conduct offensive operations against targets in cyberspace. Corporate Security, on the other hand, refers to the measures taken by organizations to protect their assets and information from unauthorized access, theft, or damage.

The relationship between Cyber Warfare and Corporate Security is complex, and it involves a number of different factors. Here are some of the ways in which the two areas are related:

Threat Landscape: Cyber Warfare and Corporate Security are both impacted by the same threat landscape. Threat actors, including nation-states, criminal organizations, hacktivists, and others, are constantly developing new tactics and techniques to infiltrate and compromise systems. This means that the same vulnerabilities that are exploited by nation-states for offensive purposes can also be exploited by criminals and other actors for financial gain or other nefarious purposes.

Attack Vectors: The attack vectors used by nation-states in Cyber Warfare can also be used by criminals and other actors in the context of Corporate Security. For example, spear-phishing attacks, malware, and ransomware can all be used to gain unauthorized access to systems and steal data. This means that organizations need to be aware of the same tactics and techniques that are used by nation-states in Cyber Warfare in order to protect themselves from other types of cyber threats.

Cybersecurity Capabilities: The same cybersecurity capabilities that are used by nation-states for offensive purposes can also be used by organizations for defensive purposes. For example, advanced threat intelligence, analytics, and other technologies can be used by organizations to detect and respond to cyber threats. This means that there is often overlap between the tools and techniques used by nation-states in Cyber Warfare and those used by organizations for Corporate Security.

Collaboration: Collaboration between the government and the private sector is essential in the context of Cyber Warfare and Corporate Security. The government has access to intelligence and other information that can be used to identify potential threats, while the private sector has the resources and expertise to implement effective security measures. Collaboration between the two is necessary to protect critical infrastructure and other assets from cyber threats.

Regulation: The government plays an important role in regulating cybersecurity in the private sector. Regulations such as the General Data Protection Regulation (GDPR) and the California Consumer Privacy Act (CCPA) require organizations to take certain steps to protect the privacy and security of personal data. These regulations are designed to protect individuals from cyber threats, but they also have an impact on the Corporate Security of organizations.

In conclusion, Cyber Warfare and Corporate Security are closely related in the context of modern cybersecurity. They are impacted by the same threat landscape, use the same attack vectors, rely on similar cybersecurity capabilities, require collaboration between the government and the private sector, and are impacted by regulation. Organizations must be aware of the threats posed by Cyber Warfare and take appropriate steps to protect their assets and information from cyber threats. At the same time, governments must work with the private sector to protect critical infrastructure and other assets from cyber threats.

Examples of Cyber Warfare affecting Corporate Security

Cyber warfare has become an increasingly prevalent threat to corporate security in recent years. The following are examples of high-profile cyber attacks that have impacted corporations and their security measures.

Target data breach (2013): In 2013, retail giant Target suffered a massive data breach that affected millions of customers' personal and financial information. The breach occurred as a result of a cyber attack on Target's payment systems, which allowed hackers to gain access to customer data. The attack highlighted the vulnerability of retailers to cyber attacks and the need for strong security measures to protect customer data.

WannaCry ransomware attack (2017): The WannaCry ransomware attack affected over 200,000 computers in more than 150 countries in May 2017. The attack targeted computers running the Microsoft Windows operating system, encrypting data and demanding payment in exchange for access. The attack impacted a number of corporations, including FedEx, Nissan, and Renault, highlighting the potential for cyber attacks to disrupt business operations and cause significant financial losses.

Equifax data breach (2017): In 2017, credit reporting agency Equifax suffered a data breach that impacted the personal information of over 143 million customers. The breach occurred as a result of a vulnerability in Equifax's website software, which allowed hackers to gain access to sensitive customer data. The incident highlighted the need for corporations to regularly assess and update their cybersecurity measures to prevent vulnerabilities from being exploited.

NotPetya malware attack (2017): The NotPetya malware attack affected corporations around the world in 2017, including shipping giant Maersk and pharmaceutical company Merck. The attack was initially thought to be a ransomware attack, but it was later discovered to be a destructive attack aimed at causing damage to computer systems and disrupting business operations. The incident demonstrated the potential for cyber attacks to cause physical damage and highlighted the need for corporations to prepare for and respond to cyber attacks effectively.

SolarWinds supply chain attack (2020): In 2020, a supply chain attack on SolarWinds, a US software company, resulted in the compromise of numerous organizations' computer systems, including US government agencies and Fortune 500 companies. The attack was carried out by a nation-state threat actor and highlighted the potential for sophisticated cyber attacks to be used as a tool of espionage and political coercion.

Conclusion:

The above examples demonstrate the potential for cyber warfare to impact corporate security in significant ways. Cyber attacks can result in the loss of sensitive information, disruption of business operations, and significant financial losses. It is essential for corporations to develop robust cybersecurity measures to protect against cyber threats and to be prepared to respond effectively to incidents when they occur. By taking these steps, corporations can better protect themselves against the increasing threat of cyber warfare.

The need for a Corporate Cybersecurity Strategy:-

In today's digital age, organizations of all sizes and types face significant cybersecurity challenges. Cyber threats such as phishing attacks, ransomware, and data breaches are on the rise, and they pose a serious risk to businesses of all kinds. To address these challenges, organizations need to develop a comprehensive Corporate Cybersecurity Strategy.

A Corporate Cybersecurity Strategy is a plan that outlines how an organization will protect its assets and information from cyber threats. The strategy should be developed in collaboration with all relevant stakeholders, including IT, legal, compliance, and business leaders. Here are some reasons why a Corporate Cybersecurity Strategy is essential for organizations:

Protecting Critical Assets: A Corporate Cybersecurity Strategy helps organizations protect their critical assets, such as customer data, financial information, and intellectual property. By identifying these assets and implementing appropriate controls, organizations can minimize the risk of data breaches, cyber attacks, and other threats.

Compliance: Many organizations are subject to regulatory requirements related to cybersecurity. For example, the General Data Protection Regulation (GDPR) requires organizations to protect the personal data of EU citizens. A Corporate Cybersecurity Strategy can help organizations comply with these requirements by identifying the controls that need to be put in place to protect personal data and other sensitive information.

Reputation: A cybersecurity breach can have a significant impact on an organization's reputation. Customers may lose trust in the organization if their data is compromised, and this can lead to a loss of business. A Corporate Cybersecurity Strategy can help organizations minimize the risk of a breach and demonstrate to customers that they take cybersecurity seriously.

Cost Savings: Cybersecurity incidents can be expensive for organizations. The cost of remediation, legal fees, and regulatory fines can add up quickly. A Corporate Cybersecurity Strategy can help organizations reduce the risk of a cybersecurity incident and save money in the long run.

Business Continuity: A cybersecurity incident can disrupt an organization's operations, leading to downtime and lost productivity. A Corporate Cybersecurity Strategy can help organizations develop plans to ensure business continuity in the event of a cyber attack or other incident.

Developing a Corporate Cybersecurity Strategy involves several steps, including:

Risk Assessment: Organizations should conduct a thorough risk assessment to identify potential threats and vulnerabilities. This should involve a review of existing controls, policies, and procedures, as well as an analysis of the threat landscape.

Governance: Organizations should establish a governance framework to oversee the development and implementation of the Corporate Cybersecurity Strategy. This should include the appointment of a Chief Information Security Officer (CISO) or equivalent, who will be responsible for cybersecurity.

Policies and Procedures: Organizations should develop and implement policies and procedures to support the Corporate Cybersecurity Strategy. This should include policies related to access control, data protection, incident response, and other areas.

Training and Awareness: Organizations should provide training and awareness programs to ensure that employees understand their role in protecting the organization's assets and information from cyber threats.

Technology: Organizations should implement appropriate technology solutions to support the Corporate Cybersecurity Strategy. This may include firewalls, intrusion detection systems, and endpoint protection solutions.

In conclusion, a Corporate Cybersecurity Strategy is essential for organizations of all sizes and types. By developing a comprehensive strategy that addresses the unique cybersecurity challenges facing the organization, organizations can protect their critical assets, comply with regulatory requirements, maintain their reputation, save costs, and ensure business continuity. Developing a Corporate Cybersecurity Strategy involves several steps, including risk assessment, governance, policies and procedures, training and awareness, and technology.

TEN

CYBER WARFARE AND CRITICAL INFRASTRUCTURE

Critical infrastructure refers to the physical and digital systems that are essential for the functioning of society, including power grids, transportation systems, and communication networks. Cyber warfare poses a significant threat to critical infrastructure, as attacks on these systems can result in significant disruption and damage. This chapter will explore the ways in which cyber warfare can impact critical infrastructure and the measures that can be taken to protect these systems.

Types of critical infrastructure:

Critical infrastructure can be divided into various categories, including:

a. Energy infrastructure: This includes power grids, oil and gas pipelines, and nuclear power plants.

b. Transportation infrastructure: This includes airports, seaports, and railways.

c. Communication infrastructure: This includes telephone and internet networks.

d. Water infrastructure: This includes water treatment plants and distribution networks.

e. Financial infrastructure: This includes banks, stock exchanges, and payment systems.

Cyber threats to critical infrastructure:

Cyber threats to critical infrastructure can take various forms, including:

a. Denial-of-service (DoS) attacks: These attacks overload a system with traffic, making it inaccessible to users.

b. Malware attacks: These attacks involve the use of malicious software to gain access to a system and steal data or disrupt operations.

c. Phishing attacks: These attacks involve the use of fraudulent emails or websites to trick users into divulging sensitive information.

d. Insider threats: These involve the use of privileged access by an employee or contractor to cause harm to a system.

Examples of cyber attacks on critical infrastructure:

The following are examples of high-profile cyber attacks on critical infrastructure:

a. Stuxnet: This was a malware attack on an Iranian nuclear facility in 2010 that was believed to be carried out by the US and Israel. The attack targeted industrial control systems, causing significant damage to the facility's centrifuges.

b. Ukraine power grid attack: In 2015 and 2016, the Ukrainian power grid was targeted by a series of cyber attacks that resulted in significant power outages. The attacks were attributed to Russian state-sponsored hackers.

c. NotPetya: This was a malware attack in 2017 that targeted companies worldwide, including shipping giant Maersk and pharmaceutical company Merck. The attack was aimed at disrupting business operations and caused significant financial losses.

Measures to protect critical infrastructure:

To protect critical infrastructure against cyber threats, various measures can be taken, including:

a. Conducting regular cybersecurity risk assessments to identify vulnerabilities and develop strategies to mitigate them.

b. Implementing robust access controls to limit access to critical systems and data.

c. Developing incident response plans to effectively respond to cyber attacks when they occur.

d. Conducting regular cybersecurity training and awareness programs for employees to help them recognize and respond to cyber threats.

The role of government in protecting critical infrastructure:

Governments play a crucial role in protecting critical infrastructure against cyber threats. Governments can take various steps to ensure the protection of critical infrastructure, including:

a. Developing and implementing regulations and standards for critical infrastructure security.

b. Conducting regular cybersecurity assessments and audits of critical infrastructure to identify vulnerabilities.

c. Providing funding for critical infrastructure security initiatives.

d. Collaborating with the private sector to develop effective strategies for protecting critical infrastructure.

Conclusion:

The increasing reliance on digital systems in critical infrastructure makes these systems vulnerable to cyber attacks. Cyber attacks on critical infrastructure can result in significant disruption and damage, posing a significant threat to society. It is essential for organizations to take proactive measures to protect critical infrastructure against cyber threats, and for governments to play a leading role in developing effective cybersecurity strategies to protect critical infrastructure. By doing so, organizations and governments can better protect critical infrastructure against the increasing threat of cyber warfare.

Relationship between Cyber Warfare and Critical Infrastructure:-

In today's digital age, critical infrastructure, such as power grids, water treatment plants, and transportation systems, has become increasingly interconnected and reliant on technology. As a result, these systems have become vulnerable to cyber attacks, which could cause significant disruption and even physical damage. The relationship between cyber warfare and critical infrastructure is complex and multifaceted, and it is important for organizations and governments to understand the risks and develop strategies to mitigate them.

Cyber warfare refers to the use of technology to conduct military operations in cyberspace. This can include cyber espionage, sabotage, and disruption. Cyber attacks on critical infrastructure can have devastating consequences, as they can result in the disruption of essential services, damage to physical infrastructure, and even loss of life. Here are some of the key ways in which cyber warfare can impact critical infrastructure:

Disruption of Services: Cyber attacks can cause disruption to critical infrastructure services, such as power, water, and transportation. For example, a cyber attack on a power grid could cause a blackout, which could result in significant economic and social impacts.

Physical Damage: In some cases, cyber attacks on critical infrastructure can result in physical damage. For example, a cyber attack on a water treatment plant could cause contaminated water to be released into the system, which could pose a health risk to the public.

Economic Impact: Cyber attacks on critical infrastructure can have a significant economic impact, as they can result in the disruption of essential services and the loss of productivity. This can have ripple effects throughout the economy.

National Security: Critical infrastructure is often essential to national security, and a cyber attack on this infrastructure could compromise national security interests. For example, a cyber attack on a military base could compromise sensitive military data.

Given the potential impact of cyber attacks on critical infrastructure, it is essential for organizations and governments to take steps to mitigate the risk. Here are some of the key strategies that can be used to protect critical infrastructure from cyber attacks:

Risk Assessment: Organizations should conduct a thorough risk assessment to identify potential threats and vulnerabilities. This should involve a review of existing controls, policies, and procedures, as well as an analysis of the threat landscape.

Governance: Organizations should establish a governance framework to oversee the development and implementation of cybersecurity measures for critical infrastructure. This should include the appointment of a Chief Information Security Officer (CISO) or equivalent, who will be responsible for cybersecurity.

Policies and Procedures: Organizations should develop and implement policies and procedures to support the protection of critical infrastructure from cyber attacks. This should include policies related to access control, data protection, incident response, and other areas.

Technology: Organizations should implement appropriate technology solutions to protect critical infrastructure from cyber attacks. This may include firewalls, intrusion detection systems, and endpoint protection solutions.

Training and Awareness: Organizations should provide training and awareness programs to ensure that employees and stakeholders understand their role in protecting critical infrastructure from cyber attacks.

Collaboration and Information Sharing: Collaboration and information sharing among organizations and governments can help to identify and mitigate cyber threats to critical infrastructure.

In conclusion, the relationship between cyber warfare and critical infrastructure is complex and multifaceted. Cyber attacks on critical infrastructure can result in disruption of essential services, physical damage, economic impact, and compromise national security interests. To protect critical infrastructure from cyber attacks, organizations and governments should take steps to conduct risk assessments, establish governance frameworks, develop policies and procedures, implement appropriate technology solutions, provide training and awareness programs, and collaborate and share information. By doing so, they can minimize the risk of cyber attacks on critical infrastructure and ensure the safety and security of the public.

Examples of Cyber Warfare affecting Critical Infrastructure:-

Critical infrastructure plays a vital role in the functioning of society, providing essential services such as energy, transportation, and communication. The increasing reliance on digital systems in critical infrastructure makes these systems vulnerable to cyber attacks. Cyber attacks on critical infrastructure can result in significant disruption and damage, posing a significant threat to society. In this chapter, we will explore examples of cyber warfare affecting critical infrastructure.

Ukraine Power Grid Attack:

In December 2015, a cyber attack targeted the Ukrainian power grid, causing significant power outages. The attackers used malware to gain access to the power company's systems, and then they used this access to disrupt the power supply. The attack affected over 225,000 customers and lasted for several hours. In December 2016, a similar attack occurred, which resulted in a power outage affecting 80,000 customers. These attacks were attributed to Russian state-sponsored hackers.

Stuxnet:

Stuxnet is a well-known example of a cyber attack on critical infrastructure. In 2010, the Stuxnet worm was discovered in an Iranian nuclear facility, where it was believed to be causing significant damage to the facility's centrifuges. Stuxnet was designed to target industrial control systems, which are used to control critical infrastructure, and was believed to have been developed jointly by the US and Israel. Stuxnet demonstrated the potential for cyber attacks to cause physical damage to critical infrastructure.

NotPetya:

NotPetya is a malware attack that targeted companies worldwide in 2017, including shipping giant Maersk and pharmaceutical company Merck. The attack was aimed at disrupting business operations and caused significant financial losses. NotPetya was designed to spread rapidly across networks, and it is estimated to have caused over $10 billion in damages.

Maroochy Shire Sewage Spill:

The Maroochy Shire sewage spill is an example of a cyber attack on critical infrastructure that caused environmental damage. In 2000, a disgruntled former employee of the Maroochy Shire council gained unauthorized access to the council's computer systems and caused a sewage spill into local waterways. The spill resulted in significant environmental damage, including the death of fish and other marine life.

Saudi Aramco:

In 2012, the Saudi Arabian oil company, Saudi Aramco, was hit by a cyber attack that destroyed 35,000 computers. The attackers used malware to gain access to the company's systems and then used this access to destroy data and disrupt operations. The attack is believed to have been carried out by Iranian state-sponsored hackers.

Colonial Pipeline:

In May 2021, the Colonial Pipeline, which supplies fuel to the eastern US, was hit by a ransomware attack that caused a significant disruption to fuel supplies. The attackers used malware to gain access to the company's systems and then encrypted the company's data, demanding a ransom for its release. The attack resulted in fuel shortages and price increases across the eastern US.

These examples illustrate the potential for cyber attacks to cause significant damage to critical infrastructure, resulting in disruption to essential services and even environmental damage. The increasing reliance on digital systems in critical infrastructure means that these systems are becoming more vulnerable to cyber attacks, and it is essential for organizations to take proactive measures to protect these systems against cyber threats.

To protect critical infrastructure against cyber attacks, organizations can take various measures, such as implementing robust access controls, conducting regular cybersecurity risk assessments, and developing incident response plans. Governments also play a crucial role in protecting critical infrastructure by developing regulations and standards for critical infrastructure security, conducting regular cybersecurity assessments and audits of critical infrastructure, and collaborating with the private sector to develop effective strategies for protecting critical infrastructure.

The need for a Critical Infrastructure Cybersecurity Strategy:-

Critical infrastructure plays a vital role in modern society, providing essential services such as electricity, water, transportation, and communication. However, the increased reliance on technology has made these systems vulnerable to cyber attacks, which can have devastating consequences. To address these risks, it is essential to have a critical infrastructure cybersecurity strategy in place.

A critical infrastructure cybersecurity strategy is a comprehensive plan for protecting critical infrastructure from cyber threats. This strategy should address the unique challenges of securing critical infrastructure, including the need for continuous availability of services, the use of legacy systems, and the complexity of managing large-scale operations. Here are some of the key components of a critical infrastructure cybersecurity strategy:

Risk Assessment: A critical infrastructure cybersecurity strategy should begin with a risk assessment to identify potential threats and vulnerabilities. This should involve a comprehensive review of existing controls, policies, and procedures, as well as an analysis of the threat landscape.

Governance: A critical infrastructure cybersecurity strategy should establish a governance framework to oversee the development and implementation of cybersecurity measures. This should include the appointment of a Chief Information Security Officer (CISO) or equivalent, who will be responsible for cybersecurity.

Policies and Procedures: A critical infrastructure cybersecurity strategy should include policies and procedures to support the protection of critical infrastructure from cyber attacks. This should include policies related to access control, data protection, incident response, and other areas.

Technology: A critical infrastructure cybersecurity strategy should include appropriate technology solutions to protect critical infrastructure from cyber attacks. This may include firewalls, intrusion detection systems, and endpoint protection solutions.

Training and Awareness: A critical infrastructure cybersecurity strategy should provide training and awareness programs to ensure that employees and stakeholders understand their role in protecting critical infrastructure from cyber attacks.

Collaboration and Information Sharing: A critical infrastructure cybersecurity strategy should promote collaboration and information sharing among organizations and governments to identify and mitigate cyber threats.

Continuous Monitoring and Improvement: A critical infrastructure cybersecurity strategy should include a continuous monitoring and improvement process to ensure that cybersecurity measures remain effective and up to date.

The development and implementation of a critical infrastructure cybersecurity strategy can help to minimize the risk of cyber attacks on critical infrastructure and ensure the safety and security of the public. Here are some of the key benefits of having a critical infrastructure cybersecurity strategy:

Protection of Essential Services: A critical infrastructure cybersecurity strategy can help to protect essential services from disruption and downtime, ensuring that these services remain available to the public.

Prevention of Physical Damage: A critical infrastructure cybersecurity strategy can help to prevent physical damage to critical infrastructure, which can have significant economic and social impacts.

Protection of National Security: Critical infrastructure is often essential to national security, and a cyber attack on this infrastructure could compromise national security interests. A critical infrastructure cybersecurity strategy can help to protect against these risks.

Compliance with Regulations: Many industries are subject to regulatory requirements for cybersecurity, and a critical infrastructure cybersecurity strategy can help to ensure compliance with these regulations.

Improved Resilience: A critical infrastructure cybersecurity strategy can help to improve the resilience of critical infrastructure, enabling it to withstand cyber attacks and recover quickly from any damage.

In conclusion, a critical infrastructure cybersecurity strategy is essential for protecting critical infrastructure from cyber threats. This strategy should include a risk assessment, governance framework, policies and procedures, technology solutions, training and awareness programs, collaboration and information sharing, and continuous monitoring and improvement. By developing and implementing a comprehensive critical infrastructure cybersecurity strategy, organizations and governments can ensure the safety and security of the public and protect essential services from cyber attacks.

ELEVEN

CYBER WARFARE AND CYBER DEFENSE

Introduction

As the prevalence and severity of cyber attacks continue to increase, the importance of cyber defense has become increasingly evident. In this chapter, we will explore the various techniques and strategies used in cyber defense to protect against cyber warfare.

Cyber Defense Strategies

The first step in cyber defense is to develop a comprehensive strategy to protect against cyber attacks. There are several strategies that organizations can employ, including:

Defense in Depth: This approach involves implementing multiple layers of security measures to protect against cyber attacks. This includes everything from firewalls and intrusion detection systems to access controls and encryption.

Cyber Threat Intelligence: By leveraging threat intelligence, organizations can gain insight into the latest tactics and techniques used by cyber criminals and nation-state actors. This information can be used to proactively identify and mitigate potential cyber threats.

Incident Response Planning: In the event of a cyber attack, it is critical to have an incident response plan in place. This includes having a team of experts who can quickly identify and respond to the attack, as well as processes for communication and collaboration with internal and external stakeholders.

Employee Education and Training: One of the most common ways that cyber attackers gain access to networks is through social engineering attacks that target employees. By providing regular education and training to employees, organizations can help to mitigate this risk.

Continuous Monitoring: Cyber attackers are constantly evolving their tactics and techniques, which means that organizations must be vigilant in their monitoring and response efforts. This includes implementing continuous monitoring and threat detection tools to identify potential threats in real-time.

Cyber Defense Technologies

In addition to implementing comprehensive cyber defense strategies, organizations must also invest in the latest technologies to protect against cyber threats. Some of the key technologies that can be used to enhance cyber defense include:

Artificial Intelligence and Machine Learning: These technologies can be used to analyze vast amounts of data to identify potential cyber threats and proactively respond to them.

Next-Generation Firewalls: These firewalls leverage advanced threat detection capabilities to identify and block potential threats.

Intrusion Prevention Systems: These systems can detect and prevent attacks by identifying suspicious activity and blocking access to potentially malicious websites and IP addresses.

Security Information and Event Management (SIEM) Tools: These tools can be used to collect and analyze data from various security sources to identify potential threats and provide real-time alerts.

Endpoint Protection: Endpoint protection tools are designed to protect individual devices such as laptops, smartphones, and tablets from cyber threats. These tools typically include features such as antivirus and anti-malware protection, as well as advanced threat detection capabilities.

Conclusion

As cyber attacks continue to increase in frequency and severity, it is critical for organizations to prioritize cyber defense efforts. By implementing comprehensive strategies and investing in the latest technologies, organizations can help to mitigate the risk of cyber attacks and protect critical assets and infrastructure. However, it is important to recognize that cyber attackers are constantly evolving their tactics and techniques, which means that organizations must remain vigilant in their cyber defense efforts and be prepared to adapt to new threats as they emerge.

Relationship between Cyber Warfare and Cyber Defense:-

The relationship between cyber warfare and cyber defense is complex and constantly evolving. Cyber warfare refers to the use of technology to conduct attacks against a country, organization, or individual, while cyber defense refers to the measures put in place to protect against these attacks. As technology continues to advance, both cyber warfare and cyber defense are becoming increasingly sophisticated, and the need for effective cyber defense is more critical than ever.

The following are some of the ways that cyber warfare and cyber defense are related:

Offensive and Defensive Tactics: Just as in traditional warfare, cyber warfare involves offensive tactics aimed at disrupting or damaging an adversary's infrastructure or data. Conversely, cyber defense involves defensive tactics aimed at detecting and preventing cyber attacks.

Technology Development: The development of new technologies drives both cyber warfare and cyber defense. As new threats emerge, defenders must develop new tools and strategies to combat them. At the same time, attackers are constantly developing new methods to evade detection and penetrate defenses.

Intelligence Gathering: Both cyber warfare and cyber defense require extensive intelligence gathering. Attackers must gather intelligence on their targets to identify vulnerabilities and develop effective attack strategies, while defenders must gather intelligence on potential threats to detect and prevent attacks.

Human Factors: Cyber warfare and cyber defense are not just about technology; they also involve human factors such as social engineering, insider threats, and human error. Attackers may use social engineering tactics to trick people into revealing sensitive information, while defenders must train employees to recognize and avoid these tactics.

National Security: Cyber warfare and cyber defense are increasingly important components of national security. Countries are investing heavily in cyber capabilities and developing offensive and defensive strategies to protect their infrastructure and citizens.

Economic Impacts: Cyber warfare and cyber defense also have significant economic impacts. Cyber attacks can cause significant financial losses for businesses and governments, while effective cyber defense can protect against these losses and help to maintain economic stability.

International Relations: Cyber warfare and cyber defense can also have implications for international relations. Countries may view cyber attacks as a form of aggression and respond with diplomatic or even military actions. International cooperation is essential to prevent cyber attacks and promote cyber defense.

In conclusion, the relationship between cyber warfare and cyber defense is complex and multifaceted. Both are constantly evolving as technology advances, and both have significant implications for national security, economic stability, and international relations. Effective cyber defense is essential to protect against cyber attacks and maintain the security and stability of our increasingly interconnected world. It requires a comprehensive approach that addresses both technology and human factors and emphasizes intelligence gathering, collaboration, and continuous improvement.

Examples of Cyber Defense Strategies

Examples of Cyber Defense Strategies

In this section, we will explore some examples of how organizations have implemented cyber defense strategies to protect against cyber attacks.

Defense in Depth: The U.S. Department of Defense (DoD) is a prime example of an organization that has implemented a defense-in-depth strategy. The DoD uses multiple layers of security measures to protect against cyber attacks, including firewalls, intrusion detection systems, access controls, encryption, and more. Additionally, the DoD conducts regular penetration testing to identify potential vulnerabilities in its defenses.

Cyber Threat Intelligence: Many organizations, including financial institutions and government agencies, have invested in cyber threat intelligence to proactively identify and mitigate potential cyber threats. For example, the Financial Services Information Sharing and Analysis Center (FS-ISAC) provides real-time threat intelligence to its members, enabling them to quickly respond to potential threats.

Incident Response Planning: In 2017, the city of Atlanta fell victim to a ransomware attack that paralyzed its operations for several days. The attack highlighted the importance of having an incident response plan in place. Following the attack, the city of Atlanta developed a comprehensive incident response plan that included a team of experts who could quickly identify and respond to potential cyber threats.

Employee Education and Training: The U.S. Department of Homeland Security (DHS) has launched several initiatives aimed at educating and training employees on cyber security best practices.

For example, the DHS Cybersecurity and Infrastructure Security Agency (CISA) offers a range of training programs, including the Federal Virtual Training Environment (FedVTE) platform, which provides free online courses on topics such as cyber security and incident response.

Continuous Monitoring: The State of Michigan is an example of an organization that has implemented continuous monitoring and threat detection tools to identify potential cyber threats. The state's Michigan Cyber Range is a virtual training ground that simulates real-world cyber attacks, enabling organizations to test their defenses and identify potential vulnerabilities. Additionally, the state uses advanced threat detection tools to monitor its networks and detect potential threats in real-time.

Conclusion

Implementing effective cyber defense strategies is critical for protecting against the growing threat of cyber attacks. By leveraging technologies and strategies such as defense in depth, cyber threat intelligence, incident response planning, employee education and training, and continuous monitoring, organizations can mitigate the risk of cyber attacks and protect their critical assets and infrastructure. However, it is important to recognize that cyber attackers are constantly evolving their tactics and techniques, which means that organizations must remain vigilant and prepared to adapt to new threats as they emerge.

The need for a Cyber Defense Strategy

In today's digital age, cyber attacks are becoming increasingly frequent, sophisticated, and damaging. As a result, organizations of all sizes and industries must develop effective cyber defense strategies to protect against these threats. A cyber defense strategy is a comprehensive approach that outlines how an organization will detect, prevent, and respond to cyber attacks.

The following are some of the reasons why a cyber defense strategy is essential:

Protecting Sensitive Information: Cyber attacks can result in the theft of sensitive information such as personal data, financial information, and intellectual property. A cyber defense strategy can help an organization to identify and protect sensitive information, preventing it from falling into the wrong hands.

Maintaining Operations: Cyber attacks can disrupt an organization's operations, causing downtime and lost revenue. A cyber defense strategy can help to ensure that critical systems remain operational in the event of an attack, minimizing the impact on business operations.

Complying with Regulations: Many industries are subject to regulations that require them to protect sensitive data and maintain certain cybersecurity standards. A cyber defense strategy can help an organization to comply with these regulations and avoid costly fines and legal action.

Protecting Reputation: Cyber attacks can damage an organization's reputation, eroding trust among customers, partners, and stakeholders. A cyber defense strategy can help to protect an organization's reputation by demonstrating a commitment to cybersecurity and protecting against attacks.

Supporting Business Growth: A strong cyber defense strategy can help to support business growth by ensuring that critical systems are secure and protected. This can give customers and partners the confidence to do business with the organization and help to drive growth.

Developing a Cyber Defense Strategy

To develop an effective cyber defense strategy, an organization must take a comprehensive approach that addresses people, processes, and technology. The following are some of the key components of a cyber defense strategy:

Risk Assessment: A risk assessment is a critical first step in developing a cyber defense strategy. It involves identifying potential threats and vulnerabilities, assessing the likelihood of an attack, and determining the potential impact of an attack.

Security Policies and Procedures: A cyber defense strategy should include comprehensive security policies and procedures that outline how the organization will protect sensitive information and respond to cyber attacks. This should include policies for password management, data encryption, and incident response.

Employee Training: Employees are often the weakest link in an organization's cyber defense. A cyber defense strategy should include comprehensive employee training on cybersecurity best practices, including how to identify and report potential threats.

Network Security: A cyber defense strategy should include robust network security measures, such as firewalls, intrusion detection systems, and anti-virus software.

Incident Response Plan: An incident response plan is a critical component of a cyber defense strategy. It outlines how the organization will respond to a cyber attack, including who will be responsible for each step of the response, how communications will be handled, and what steps will be taken to restore systems and data.

Continuous Improvement: A cyber defense strategy is not a one-time event; it must be an ongoing process of continuous improvement. This involves regularly assessing the effectiveness of security measures, monitoring for new threats, and updating policies and procedures as necessary.

Conclusion

In today's digital age, the threat of cyber attacks is constant and evolving. Developing a comprehensive cyber defense strategy is essential for protecting an organization's sensitive information, maintaining operations, complying with regulations, and protecting reputation. A cyber defense strategy should take a comprehensive approach that addresses people, processes, and technology, including risk assessment, security policies and procedures, employee training, network security, incident response, and continuous improvement. By prioritizing cybersecurity and developing a strong defense strategy, organizations can protect themselves against the growing threat of cyber attacks.

TWELVE

The Role of Government in Cyber Warfare

In the modern era, the role of governments in cyber warfare is a subject of intense scrutiny and debate. In this chapter, we will explore the various ways in which governments around the world are involved in cyber warfare and the implications of their actions.

Government's Role in Cyber Warfare

Governments have many different roles in cyber warfare, ranging from developing offensive capabilities to defending their own infrastructure. Some of the primary ways in which governments are involved in cyber warfare include:

Offensive Cyber Operations: Governments around the world have developed offensive cyber capabilities that can be used to disrupt, degrade, or destroy the information systems of their adversaries. These capabilities may include malware, denial-of-service attacks, and other techniques designed to compromise or destroy information systems.

Defensive Cyber Operations: Governments are also involved in defensive cyber operations, including the development of technologies and strategies to protect their own infrastructure and networks from cyber attacks. This may include the use of firewalls, intrusion detection systems, and other technologies designed to detect and respond to cyber threats.

Cyber Espionage: Governments around the world engage in cyber espionage, which involves the covert gathering of intelligence through the use of cyber tools and techniques. This may involve the use of malware, phishing attacks, or other methods to infiltrate the networks of foreign governments or organizations.

Cyber Diplomacy: In recent years, governments have also become involved in cyber diplomacy, which involves the use of diplomatic channels to address cyber security issues and establish norms for behavior in cyberspace.

Implications of Government Involvement in Cyber Warfare

The involvement of governments in cyber warfare raises many legal, ethical, and strategic considerations. Some of the key implications of government involvement in cyber warfare include:

International Law: The use of cyber operations in warfare raises important questions about the applicability of international law, including the law of armed conflict, to cyber operations. Many experts believe that existing international law is inadequate to address the unique challenges posed by cyber warfare, which means that new legal frameworks may be needed.

National Security: Governments must balance the need to protect their own infrastructure and citizens from cyber threats with the need to respect civil liberties and human rights. This can be a difficult balancing act, particularly in the case of offensive cyber operations, which may involve the use of intrusive or illegal techniques.

Cyber Deterrence: The use of cyber operations in warfare also raises questions about deterrence. Traditional methods of deterrence, such as the threat of military force, may be less effective in the cyber domain, which means that new methods of deterrence may be needed.

International Relations: The involvement of governments in cyber warfare can also have important implications for international relations. The use of cyber operations against foreign governments or organizations can create diplomatic tensions and raise concerns about the use of force in cyberspace.

Conclusion

The role of governments in cyber warfare is complex and multifaceted. Governments have many different roles in cyber warfare, including the development of offensive and defensive capabilities, cyber espionage, and cyber diplomacy. The involvement of governments in cyber warfare raises important legal, ethical, and strategic considerations, including questions about the applicability of international law, the balance between national security and civil liberties, the effectiveness of deterrence, and the impact on international relations. As cyberspace continues to evolve, it will be important for governments to adapt their strategies and policies to address these challenges and ensure the safety and security of their citizens and critical infrastructure.

Role of government in Cyber Warfare

In the modern era, governments around the world recognize the importance of cybersecurity and its implications on national security. With the rise of cyber warfare, governments play a vital role in ensuring the protection of their critical infrastructure, defense networks, and sensitive information from potential cyber attacks. This article explores the role of the government in cyber warfare and its importance in maintaining the security of the nation.

National Security Policy

Governments around the world formulate national security policies that aim to protect their country from both external and internal threats. In today's digital age, these policies must include provisions to protect against cyber threats. Governments are responsible for formulating and enforcing cybersecurity policies and guidelines to protect critical infrastructure, defense networks, and sensitive information.

Cyber Intelligence

Cyber intelligence is crucial for identifying and preventing potential cyber threats. Governments have a critical role in cyber intelligence by providing resources, technology, and training to their intelligence agencies. The government also coordinates with other intelligence agencies across the world to gather and share information about potential threats.

Cyber Defense

Governments are responsible for protecting their critical infrastructure and defense networks from cyber attacks. Governments use various cybersecurity measures to ensure their networks are protected, such as firewalls, intrusion detection systems, and antivirus software. The government also works with private companies to ensure that they implement appropriate cybersecurity measures.

Offensive Cyber Operations

Governments may also engage in offensive cyber operations to protect national security interests. Offensive cyber operations involve hacking into the systems of other countries or groups to gain intelligence or disrupt their operations. These operations are typically carried out by intelligence agencies or military organizations.

International Cooperation

International cooperation is vital in the fight against cyber threats. Governments must work together to share information and coordinate their efforts to prevent cyber attacks. International agreements, such as the Budapest Convention on Cybercrime, provide a framework for countries to work together to combat cybercrime.

Legislation and Regulation

Governments can also create legislation and regulations to improve cybersecurity. For example, the European Union's General Data Protection Regulation (GDPR) requires companies to protect the personal data of EU citizens. The U.S. government has also created regulations, such as the Federal Information Security Modernization Act (FISMA), to ensure that government agencies implement appropriate cybersecurity measures.

Cyber Diplomacy

Cyber diplomacy involves using diplomatic channels to address cyber issues. Governments may engage in cyber diplomacy to negotiate agreements with other countries or to address cybercrime committed by foreign nationals. For example, in 2015, the U.S. and China signed an agreement not to engage in economic espionage through cyberspace.

Cybersecurity Education

Finally, the government plays a critical role in promoting cybersecurity education. Governments can provide funding for research and development in cybersecurity, as well as educational programs to train the next generation of cybersecurity professionals. The government can also work with private companies to promote cybersecurity awareness and education among the general public.

Conclusion

Governments play a critical role in ensuring cybersecurity and protecting national security interests. The government is responsible for formulating and enforcing national security policies, gathering and sharing cyber intelligence, protecting critical infrastructure and defense networks, engaging in offensive cyber operations when necessary, cooperating with other countries to combat cyber threats, creating legislation and regulations to improve cybersecurity, engaging in cyber diplomacy, and promoting cybersecurity education. By taking these steps, governments can protect their citizens and ensure the security of the nation in an increasingly digital world

Examples of government initiatives in Cyber Warfare

Governments around the world have recognized the importance of cyber warfare and have taken steps to develop initiatives aimed at protecting their countries and their citizens from cyber attacks. Here are some examples of government initiatives in cyber warfare:

United States Cyber Command (USCYBERCOM): Established in 2009, USCYBERCOM is a unified command under the United States Department of Defense that is responsible for defending the country against cyber attacks. It is also responsible for planning and executing offensive cyber operations.

United Kingdom National Cyber Security Centre (NCSC): The NCSC is part of the Government Communications Headquarters (GCHQ) and is responsible for protecting the UK against cyber attacks. The NCSC provides advice and guidance to businesses and individuals on how to stay safe online.

Australian Cyber Security Centre (ACSC): The ACSC is part of the Australian Signals Directorate (ASD) and is responsible for providing cyber security advice and assistance to the Australian government, businesses, and individuals. The ACSC also coordinates the country's response to cyber incidents.

European Union Agency for Cybersecurity (ENISA): ENISA is an agency of the European Union that is responsible for ensuring a high level of network and information security within the EU. It provides advice and guidance to EU member states on how to protect their networks and systems from cyber attacks.

Chinese Cybersecurity Law: In 2017, China enacted a new cybersecurity law that requires all network operators in the country to store user data within China and to cooperate with the government in matters related to national security. The law also includes provisions aimed at protecting critical infrastructure from cyber attacks.

Israel National Cyber Directorate (INCD): The INCD is responsible for protecting Israel against cyber attacks and for promoting the country's cybersecurity industry. It provides guidance to government agencies, critical infrastructure providers, and businesses on how to protect their networks and systems from cyber threats.

Canadian Centre for Cyber Security (CCCS): The CCCS is part of the Communications Security Establishment (CSE) and is responsible for protecting the country against cyber attacks. It provides advice and guidance to government agencies, critical infrastructure providers, and businesses on how to protect their networks and systems from cyber threats.

Indian Computer Emergency Response Team (CERT-In): CERT-In is a government agency that is responsible for protecting India against cyber attacks. It provides advice and guidance to government agencies, critical infrastructure providers, and businesses on how to protect their networks and systems from cyber threats.

South Korean Cyber Command: Established in 2010, the South Korean Cyber Command is responsible for protecting the country against cyber attacks. It is also responsible for conducting offensive cyber operations against North Korea.

Russian National Coordination Centre for Computer Incidents (NCCC): The NCCC is a government agency that is responsible for protecting Russia against cyber attacks. It provides guidance to government agencies, critical infrastructure providers, and businesses on how to protect their networks and systems from cyber threats.

These are just a few examples of the initiatives that governments around the world have taken to protect their countries and their citizens from cyber attacks. As the threat of cyber warfare continues to grow, it is likely that more countries will develop similar initiatives to defend against this emerging threat.

The need for collaboration between governments

In the digital age, countries are increasingly interconnected, and cyber threats do not recognize borders. As a result, collaboration between governments is critical to preventing and mitigating cyber threats. This article explores the need for collaboration between governments in the fight against cyber threats and the benefits of working together.

Shared Threats

Cyber threats are not limited to one country or region. Hackers and cybercriminals can target any country with an internet connection, and attacks can have severe consequences. By collaborating with other governments, countries can share information about potential threats and work together to develop solutions.

Coordination of Response

In the event of a cyber attack, governments must work together to respond quickly and effectively. Collaboration between governments can help ensure that responses are coordinated and that resources are deployed effectively. For example, in 2017, the WannaCry ransomware attack affected computers in over 150 countries. Collaboration between governments was critical in mitigating the effects of the attack.

Pooling of Resources

Cybersecurity is an expensive endeavor, requiring significant investments in technology, training, and personnel. Collaboration between governments can help countries pool their resources and share the costs of cybersecurity. This can be particularly beneficial for smaller countries with limited resources.

International Agreements

International agreements and treaties can provide a framework for collaboration between governments. The Budapest Convention on Cybercrime, for example, provides a basis for countries to work together to combat cybercrime. By ratifying such agreements, countries commit to collaborating with other countries in the fight against cyber threats.

Intelligence Sharing

Cyber intelligence is crucial for identifying and preventing cyber threats. Governments have a critical role in cyber intelligence by providing resources, technology, and training to their intelligence agencies. The government also coordinates with other intelligence agencies across the world to gather and share information about potential threats. By collaborating on intelligence sharing, countries can increase their understanding of potential threats and better protect against them.

Coordinated Defense

Governments can also work together to develop coordinated defense strategies. By sharing information about potential threats and coordinating their response, countries can better protect their critical infrastructure, defense networks, and sensitive information. This can be particularly important in the event of a large-scale cyber attack that affects multiple countries.

Cyber Diplomacy

Finally, collaboration between governments can help promote cyber diplomacy. Cyber diplomacy involves using diplomatic channels to address cyber issues. Governments may engage in cyber diplomacy to negotiate agreements with other countries or to address cybercrime committed by foreign nationals. By working together, countries can build trust and improve cooperation in the fight against cyber threats.

Conclusion

In conclusion, collaboration between governments is critical to preventing and mitigating cyber threats. By working together, countries can share information, coordinate responses, pool resources, and develop coordinated defense strategies. International agreements and treaties can provide a framework for collaboration, while cyber intelligence sharing can increase understanding of potential threats. By promoting cyber diplomacy, countries can build trust and improve cooperation in the fight against cyber threats.

THIRTEEN

CYBER WARFARE AND THE MILITARY

The military has always been at the forefront of defending a country's interests and protecting its citizens. In today's digital age, the military's role in defending a country has expanded to include cyber warfare. Cyber warfare has become an essential component of modern warfare, and the military's role in it cannot be overstated. This chapter will explore the role of the military in cyber warfare and the challenges they face.

Role of the Military in Cyber Warfare:

The military's role in cyber warfare is to provide security and protect critical infrastructure, including government networks, communication systems, and military equipment, from cyber-attacks. Military cyber warfare units are responsible for identifying, investigating, and mitigating cyber threats to national security. These units work closely with other government agencies, such as the National Security Agency (NSA) and the Department of Homeland Security (DHS), to ensure that the country is adequately protected against cyber threats.

In addition to protecting national security, the military also uses cyber warfare as a tool for offense. Cyber-attacks can be used to disrupt an enemy's communication systems, disable their weapons systems, or infiltrate their networks to gain critical information.

The military cyber units are tasked with developing and executing offensive cyber operations against enemy targets. Offensive cyber operations require a high degree of skill and expertise, and the military invests heavily in training and equipment to ensure that its cyber warfare capabilities remain state-of-the-art.

Challenges faced by the Military in Cyber Warfare:

The military faces several challenges in executing cyber warfare operations. One of the primary challenges is the dynamic and rapidly changing nature of cyber threats. Cyber threats evolve constantly, and the military must keep up with these changes to remain effective. This requires ongoing investment in research and development to ensure that the military's cyber warfare capabilities remain up to date.

Another challenge is the need for collaboration and coordination with other government agencies, private companies, and international partners. Cyber threats are not limited by borders, and an effective response requires cooperation and collaboration with other countries and entities. This requires a high degree of trust and sharing of sensitive information, which can be difficult to achieve.

The military also faces challenges in recruiting and retaining highly skilled cyber professionals. Cybersecurity professionals are in high demand, and the military must compete with private industry for talent. Additionally, the military's strict regulations and procedures can make it difficult to attract and retain cyber professionals who prefer a more flexible and less hierarchical work environment.

Examples of Military Cyber Warfare Operations:

The military has executed several cyber warfare operations over the years. One of the most well-known examples is the Stuxnet virus, which was used to attack Iran's nuclear program. Stuxnet was designed to infiltrate and damage centrifuges used to enrich uranium, effectively sabotaging Iran's nuclear program.

Another example is the cyber-attack on the Ukrainian power grid in 2015. Russian hackers were able to gain access to the power grid's control systems, which allowed them to remotely shut down power to more than 200,000 people. The attack was a clear demonstration of the military's ability to use cyber warfare to disrupt critical infrastructure.

Conclusion:

In conclusion, the military's role in cyber warfare is essential to protecting a country's national security and critical infrastructure. The military has the responsibility of protecting the country from cyber-attacks and using cyber warfare as a tool for offense when necessary. However, the military faces several challenges in executing cyber warfare operations, including the rapidly changing nature of cyber threats, the need for collaboration and coordination with other entities, and the recruitment and retention of highly skilled cyber professionals. Despite these challenges, the military remains at the forefront of cyber warfare, and its cyber capabilities are critical to a country's overall defense strategy.

Relationship between Cyber Warfare and the Military

Cyber warfare has become a critical element of modern military operations. With the increasing reliance on technology in warfare, military forces must be prepared to defend against cyber attacks and use cyber capabilities to support their operations. In this article, we will explore the relationship between cyber warfare and the military, and how the military has evolved to meet the challenges posed by cyber threats.

The Role of Cyber Warfare in Military Operations

Cyber warfare has become a key component of modern military operations. Military forces around the world rely on technology to support their operations, and cyber attacks can have severe consequences for their ability to function effectively. Cyber warfare can be used to disrupt communications networks, disable critical infrastructure, and compromise sensitive information.

In addition to defense against cyber attacks, militaries can also use cyber capabilities to support their operations. Cyber operations can be used to gather intelligence, disrupt enemy communications, and disable enemy infrastructure. As such, cyber capabilities have become an essential tool for military forces around the world.

The Need for Cybersecurity in the Military

With the increasing reliance on technology in military operations, cybersecurity has become a critical concern for militaries around the world. Cyber attacks can compromise sensitive information, disrupt communications networks, and disable critical infrastructure. As such, militaries must have robust cybersecurity measures in place to defend against cyber threats.

Militaries must also be prepared to respond quickly and effectively in the event of a cyber attack. This requires regular training and simulation exercises to ensure that personnel are prepared to respond to cyber threats.

The Evolution of Military Doctrine

As cyber threats have become more prevalent, militaries around the world have evolved their doctrine to incorporate cyber capabilities into their operations. Many militaries have established dedicated cyber units to develop and deploy cyber capabilities.

In addition to developing cyber capabilities, militaries have also recognized the importance of international cooperation in the fight against cyber threats. Many militaries engage in joint training exercises and share information with their counterparts around the world.

Cyber Warfare and International Law

The use of cyber capabilities in military operations raises significant legal questions. International law is still developing in this area, and there is ongoing debate about what constitutes a legitimate use of cyber capabilities in military operations.

The Tallinn Manual, published by the NATO Cooperative Cyber Defence Centre of Excellence, provides guidance on the application of international law to cyber warfare. The manual sets out rules and principles for the conduct of cyber warfare, including the principles of distinction, proportionality, and necessity.

The Future of Cyber Warfare and the Military

As technology continues to evolve, so too will the role of cyber warfare in military operations. Militaries will continue to develop and deploy cyber capabilities, and cybersecurity will remain a critical concern.

The development of artificial intelligence (AI) and machine learning (ML) will also have significant implications for cyber warfare. AI and ML can be used to automate cyber operations, making them faster and more efficient.

However, as with any technology, AI and ML also pose significant risks. These technologies can be used to automate attacks, making them more difficult to defend against. As such, militaries must continue to adapt and evolve their cybersecurity measures to keep pace with these developments.

Conclusion

In conclusion, cyber warfare has become a critical element of modern military operations. Militaries must be prepared to defend against cyber attacks and use cyber capabilities to support their operations. Robust cybersecurity measures are essential to protect against cyber threats, and the evolution of military doctrine reflects the increasing importance of cyber capabilities. The ongoing development of technology, including AI and ML, will continue to shape the role of cyber warfare in military operations in the years to come.

Examples of Military involvement in Cyber Warfare

The use of cyber operations by militaries around the world has become increasingly prevalent in recent years, with many nations establishing dedicated cyber commands and integrating cyber capabilities into their overall military strategies. Some of the notable examples of military involvement in cyber warfare are:

United States Cyber Command: The United States Cyber Command (USCYBERCOM) is one of the most prominent examples of military involvement in cyber warfare. Established in 2009,

USCYBERCOM is a unified combatant command that is responsible for conducting cyberspace operations in defense of the United States and its interests. USCYBERCOM operates in conjunction with other government agencies and private sector partners to detect, deter, and respond to cyber threats.

Chinese People's Liberation Army (PLA) Strategic Support Force: The PLA Strategic Support Force is a branch of the Chinese military that was established in 2015 to oversee China's space, cyber, and electronic warfare capabilities. The force is responsible for conducting offensive and defensive cyber operations, as well as providing support for military operations in other domains.

Russian Military Intelligence: The Russian military's involvement in cyber warfare has been widely reported, with the country accused of using cyber operations to interfere in the 2016 US presidential election, among other activities. Russian military intelligence, also known as the GRU, has been linked to various cyber attacks on government and private sector targets.

Israeli Defense Forces Unit 8200: The Israeli Defense Forces (IDF) Unit 8200 is a highly skilled intelligence unit that is responsible for gathering and analyzing intelligence from various sources, including cyber operations. The unit has been involved in several high-profile cyber operations, including the development of the Stuxnet worm, which was used to disrupt Iran's nuclear program.

United Kingdom Joint Cyber Unit: The United Kingdom Joint Cyber Unit is a collaboration between the country's intelligence agencies and the Ministry of Defence. The unit is responsible for protecting the UK's interests in cyberspace, as well as conducting offensive cyber operations when necessary.

Indian Defense Cyber Agency: The Indian Defense Cyber Agency (DCA) is a newly established organization that is responsible for defending India's military networks and infrastructure against cyber threats. The DCA is also tasked with conducting offensive cyber operations against potential adversaries.

These are just a few examples of the military's involvement in cyber warfare, but they illustrate the increasing importance of cyber capabilities in modern military operations. As cyber threats continue to evolve and become more sophisticated, it is likely that the military will play an even greater role in defending against these threats and using cyber operations as a tool for achieving strategic objectives.

The need for a Military Cybersecurity Strategy

The increasing reliance on technology and the digital infrastructure has led to the integration of cyber warfare into military operations. With the rise of cyberattacks, military organizations around the world have recognized the importance of developing and implementing effective cybersecurity strategies to protect their information systems, networks, and critical infrastructure from potential cyber threats.

The need for a military cybersecurity strategy stems from the fact that military organizations possess highly sensitive information and operate complex information systems and networks, which can be vulnerable to cyberattacks. Military operations require secure communication channels, and if these channels are compromised, it can result in severe consequences such as loss of life, damage to equipment, or the compromise of sensitive information.

A military cybersecurity strategy should address the unique threats and challenges faced by military organizations. The strategy should encompass policies, procedures, and technologies to protect military systems and networks against a range of threats, from hacking and malware attacks to insider threats and nation-state-sponsored cyberattacks.

One of the primary objectives of a military cybersecurity strategy is to ensure the confidentiality, integrity, and availability of critical information and systems. This includes protecting data at rest and in transit, securing military networks, and controlling access to sensitive information. The strategy should also include measures for incident response and recovery in the event of a cyberattack.

A military cybersecurity strategy must also take into account the unique nature of military operations, including the need for operational security (OPSEC) and information security (INFOSEC). OPSEC refers to the measures taken to prevent the disclosure of sensitive information that could be used by an adversary to exploit a military operation. INFOSEC encompasses the policies and procedures used to protect information from unauthorized access, use, disclosure, disruption, modification, or destruction.

The military also faces unique challenges in terms of managing its supply chain. A military cybersecurity strategy should include measures to ensure the security of the supply chain, including vetting suppliers and ensuring that equipment and software used in military operations are secure and free of vulnerabilities.

In addition to protecting its own systems and networks, military organizations also have a responsibility to protect critical infrastructure, both domestically and abroad. Cyberattacks against critical infrastructure, such as power grids or water treatment facilities, could have severe consequences and disrupt military operations. Therefore, a military cybersecurity strategy must also address the protection of critical infrastructure and the collaboration between the military and other government agencies responsible for its protection.

One of the critical elements of a military cybersecurity strategy is training and education. All members of the military, from high-ranking officers to frontline troops, must be aware of the risks and threats posed by cyberattacks and know how to respond to them. Cybersecurity training should be ongoing and include scenarios that simulate real-world cyberattacks.

Furthermore, military organizations must work closely with the private sector and academia to stay ahead of emerging cyber threats and technologies. Collaboration between the military, industry, and academia can help identify and address vulnerabilities and develop new technologies and strategies to protect against cyberattacks.

In conclusion, the need for a military cybersecurity strategy is essential in today's digital age. Military organizations must prioritize the development and implementation of effective cybersecurity strategies to protect their information systems, networks, and critical infrastructure from potential cyber threats. Such strategies should encompass policies, procedures, and technologies to protect military systems and networks against a range of threats, from hacking and malware attacks to insider threats and nation-state-sponsored cyberattacks. The strategy must also include measures for incident response and recovery in the event of a cyberattack and must address the unique nature of military operations, including the need for operational security (OPSEC) and information security (INFOSEC). Finally, collaboration between the military, government agencies, private sector, and academia is critical to stay ahead of emerging cyber threats and technologies.

FOURTEEN

Cyber Warfare and Diplomacy

Diplomacy plays an important role in cyber warfare, as it provides a framework for nations to communicate and negotiate about issues related to cyber threats, attacks, and defense. Cyber attacks can have significant consequences on national security, economic stability, and political relations between nations. Therefore, it is essential for nations to engage in diplomatic efforts to prevent and mitigate the impact of cyber warfare.

International cooperation and collaboration are necessary for effective diplomacy in cyber warfare. Nations need to work together to develop common standards, rules, and regulations for cyberspace. Diplomatic efforts can also promote information sharing between nations, which is essential for identifying and addressing cyber threats. In addition, diplomatic efforts can facilitate the development of international norms and agreements related to cyber warfare, which can help prevent cyber conflicts and minimize their impact.

One of the most significant challenges in cyber diplomacy is the lack of a clear legal framework governing cyber warfare. International law is still developing in this area, and many countries have different interpretations of what constitutes a cyber attack and what responses are legally justified. This lack of clarity can lead to misunderstandings and escalation of cyber conflicts, which is why diplomatic efforts are essential in promoting cooperation and understanding between nations.

Another challenge in cyber diplomacy is the issue of attribution. Cyber attacks can be difficult to trace back to their origin, which can make it challenging to identify the responsible party. This can create diplomatic tensions, as nations may blame each other for attacks without sufficient evidence. Diplomatic efforts can help mitigate these tensions by promoting cooperation and communication between nations in identifying and addressing cyber threats.

Examples of Diplomatic Efforts in Cyber Warfare:

The United Nations Group of Governmental Experts on Developments in the Field of Information and Telecommunications in the Context of International Security (UN GGE) is a group of experts from various nations that have been meeting since 2004 to discuss issues related to cyber warfare. The group has produced several reports on the topic, which have been instrumental in shaping international discussions on cyber warfare.

The Budapest Convention on Cybercrime is an international treaty that aims to address cybercrime by establishing a framework for cooperation and coordination between nations. The convention has been signed by over 60 countries and provides a framework for international cooperation in investigating and prosecuting cybercrime.

The Tallinn Manual is a non-binding document that provides guidance on how international law applies to cyber warfare. The manual was developed by an international group of experts and provides guidance on issues such as the definition of cyber warfare, the legal basis for cyber operations, and the law of armed conflict in cyberspace.

The Cybersecurity Information Sharing Act (CISA) is a law passed by the United States government in 2015, which aims to promote the sharing of cybersecurity threat information between the government and private sector. The law provides legal protection for private entities that share information with the government and encourages cooperation between the government and private sector in addressing cyber threats.

The Cybersecurity Strategy of the European Union is a strategy developed by the European Union to improve cybersecurity across the EU. The strategy includes measures to promote international cooperation on cybersecurity, improve cybersecurity standards and practices, and increase funding for cybersecurity research and development.

Conclusion:

Diplomacy plays a critical role in addressing the challenges posed by cyber warfare. International cooperation and collaboration are necessary for developing common standards, rules, and regulations for cyberspace. Diplomatic efforts can promote information sharing, facilitate the development of international norms and agreements, and help mitigate the impact of cyber conflicts. However, the lack of a clear legal framework and challenges related to attribution present significant challenges to effective diplomacy in cyber warfare. Nonetheless, continued diplomatic efforts are essential in promoting understanding and cooperation between nations in addressing cyber threats.

Relationship between Cyber Warfare and Diplomacy

In today's world, cybersecurity and diplomacy are becoming increasingly intertwined due to the significant impact that cyber operations can have on international relations. Cyber attacks can target critical infrastructure, governments, and businesses, which can lead to serious economic and political consequences. Therefore, it is crucial to consider the relationship between cyber warfare and diplomacy and the need for a diplomatic approach to address cybersecurity challenges.

Diplomacy can be defined as the art of negotiating and managing international relations through peaceful means. It involves establishing and maintaining relationships with other countries and using dialogue, treaties, and international agreements to resolve conflicts and promote cooperation. Diplomatic efforts are often necessary to address cyber warfare issues because they involve the actions of foreign nations and may affect international relations.

One example of the relationship between cyber warfare and diplomacy is the Stuxnet attack on Iran's nuclear program, which was attributed to the United States and Israel. The attack caused significant damage to Iran's nuclear facilities, and its discovery strained relations between the countries involved. Diplomatic efforts were needed to manage the fallout from the attack and to prevent a potential escalation of conflict.

Another example is the recent SolarWinds hack, which affected many U.S. government agencies and private companies. The U.S. government attributed the attack to Russia and responded with diplomatic efforts, including the expulsion of Russian diplomats and the imposition of sanctions. These actions were intended to send a message to Russia about the consequences of such attacks and to deter future cyber operations.

The relationship between cyber warfare and diplomacy is also evident in international organizations such as the United Nations. The UN has recognized the importance of cybersecurity and has taken steps to promote international cooperation on this issue. In 2015, the UN established the Group of Governmental Experts on Developments in the Field of Information and Telecommunications in the Context of International Security (GGE), which produced several reports on cybersecurity and recommended norms of behavior for states in cyberspace.

The need for a diplomatic approach to cybersecurity is clear. Cyber attacks often have political implications, and addressing them requires the involvement of multiple actors, including governments, businesses, and civil society. Diplomacy can help to establish norms of behavior in cyberspace, promote cooperation, and mitigate the risk of conflict. It can also help to ensure that cybersecurity measures do not violate human rights or undermine privacy.

A diplomatic approach to cybersecurity involves several key elements. First, it requires building trust and cooperation among nations to establish a common understanding of cybersecurity issues. This involves engaging in dialogue and information-sharing to identify threats and vulnerabilities and to develop best practices for cybersecurity.

Second, diplomacy can help to establish international norms and rules for behavior in cyberspace. This can involve the development of international agreements, such as the Budapest Convention on Cybercrime, which provides a framework for cooperation on cybercrime investigations and prosecutions.

Third, diplomacy can be used to address cyber conflict and to prevent escalation. This involves engaging in dialogue with other nations to resolve disputes and to establish mechanisms for managing cyber incidents.

Finally, a diplomatic approach to cybersecurity requires a recognition of the interconnected nature of cybersecurity issues. Cybersecurity challenges affect multiple sectors, including government, business, and civil society. Therefore, diplomatic efforts must involve a range of stakeholders to ensure that cybersecurity measures are effective and respect the rights and interests of all parties.

In conclusion, the relationship between cyber warfare and diplomacy is becoming increasingly important in today's interconnected world. Cybersecurity challenges require a diplomatic approach that involves building trust, establishing international norms, addressing conflict, and recognizing the interconnected nature of cybersecurity issues. Diplomacy can help to promote cooperation and prevent conflict, and it is essential for ensuring that cyberspace remains secure and stable.

Examples of Diplomatic efforts in Cyber Warfare

In the realm of cyber warfare, diplomacy has become an essential tool to address the challenges posed by malicious cyber activities. Countries are increasingly turning to diplomatic channels to address cyber threats, establish norms and rules of conduct, and enhance international cooperation to prevent and mitigate cyber attacks. In this chapter, we will discuss some examples of diplomatic efforts in cyber warfare.

United Nations Group of Governmental Experts (UN GGE)

The UN GGE is a forum established by the UN General Assembly in 2004 to study and make recommendations on international security issues. In 2010, the UN GGE included cybersecurity in its mandate and produced its first report in 2013, which established the first international norms for state behavior in cyberspace. The report emphasized the importance of respecting international law, including the UN Charter, and called for states to work together to prevent malicious cyber activities.

Budapest Convention on Cybercrime

The Budapest Convention is a treaty that aims to harmonize national laws on cybercrime and establish cooperation between countries to investigate and prosecute cybercrime. It was adopted in 2001 by the Council of Europe and has been ratified by over 60 countries. The Convention addresses a wide range of cyber offenses, including hacking, fraud, and online child pornography. It also requires signatories to establish national legislation criminalizing cybercrime and to cooperate with each other in investigations and prosecutions.

NATO Cooperative Cyber Defence Centre of Excellence (CCDCOE)

The CCDCOE is a NATO-affiliated institution established in 2008 to promote cyber defense cooperation and expertise among NATO and its partners. The Center conducts research, training, and exercises to enhance cyber defense capabilities and develop cyber defense policies. It also provides a platform for information exchange and collaboration among NATO members and partner countries.

Shanghai Cooperation Organization (SCO)

The SCO is a regional organization established in 2001 by China, Russia, Kazakhstan, Kyrgyzstan, Tajikistan, and Uzbekistan to address security issues in Central Asia. In recent years, the SCO has become more involved in cybersecurity issues, and its member states have established a joint agreement on cooperation in the field of international information security. The agreement aims to promote the development of international norms and rules for behavior in cyberspace and enhance cooperation in preventing and combating cyber threats.

Tallinn Manual 2.0

The Tallinn Manual is a non-binding academic study on the application of international law to cyber operations. The original Tallinn Manual was published in 2013 and focused on the legal framework for cyber warfare. In 2017, a new edition, Tallinn Manual 2.0, was published, which addressed the application of international law to cyber operations in peacetime. The Manual provides guidance on how existing international law, such as the law of armed conflict and human rights law, applies to cyber operations.

Global Commission on the Stability of Cyberspace (GCSC)

The GCSC is an international group of experts established in 2017 to develop norms and policy recommendations for promoting stability and security in cyberspace. The Commission aims to develop a common understanding of the principles and norms that should govern state behavior in cyberspace and promote their adoption by governments and other stakeholders. The Commission's work focuses on five areas: norms, confidence-building measures, capacity-building, international law, and the role of non-state actors.

In conclusion, diplomacy plays an essential role in addressing the challenges posed by cyber warfare. The examples discussed in this chapter illustrate the diverse range of diplomatic efforts underway to enhance international cooperation, establish norms and rules of conduct, and prevent and mitigate malicious cyber activities.

The need for Cyber Diplomacy

As cyber warfare continues to grow and evolve, it has become increasingly clear that traditional diplomatic channels are often insufficient to address the unique challenges presented by cyber threats. Therefore, the need for cyber diplomacy has emerged as a crucial element in international relations. Cyber diplomacy refers to the use of diplomatic channels to address issues related to cybersecurity, including the development of norms, rules, and agreements among nations to promote responsible behavior in cyberspace.

The need for cyber diplomacy is evident in the growing number of cyber attacks that are launched across national borders. These attacks can have significant consequences, including economic damage, national security threats, and threats to personal privacy. Diplomacy provides a mechanism for nations to work together to address these threats, while also ensuring that each nation's interests are protected.

Cyber diplomacy involves the development of international agreements, norms, and principles that promote responsible behavior in cyberspace. These agreements can take many forms, including treaties, declarations, and codes of conduct. For example, the Tallinn Manual, developed by the NATO Cooperative Cyber Defense Center of Excellence, outlines international legal principles for responding to cyber attacks. Similarly, the United Nations Group of Governmental Experts on Developments in the Field of Information and Telecommunications in the Context of International Security (UN GGE) has developed a series of reports that outline norms for responsible behavior in cyberspace.

The need for cyber diplomacy is also evident in the growing importance of cyber issues in international relations. Cybersecurity has become a key element of national security, and cyber attacks have the potential to create significant geopolitical risks. Therefore, it is important for nations to work together to address these threats and to promote responsible behavior in cyberspace.

The role of cyber diplomacy can also be seen in the efforts of nations to address issues related to cyber espionage. Cyber espionage involves the theft of sensitive information by one nation from another nation. This activity can create significant diplomatic tension, as nations seek to protect their national security interests while also promoting responsible behavior in cyberspace. Diplomacy provides a mechanism for nations to work together to address these issues, while also promoting transparency and mutual understanding.

In addition to promoting international agreements, cyber diplomacy also involves the development of bilateral relationships between nations. These relationships can provide a mechanism for nations to share information and best practices related to cybersecurity, and to work together to address specific cyber threats. For example, the United States and China have developed a bilateral cyber agreement that includes commitments to avoid conducting cyber-enabled theft of intellectual property.

Finally, the need for cyber diplomacy is evident in the growing importance of international organizations in addressing cyber threats. These organizations, including the United Nations, the International Telecommunication Union, and NATO, can provide a mechanism for nations to work together to address cyber threats and to promote responsible behavior in cyberspace.

In conclusion, cyber diplomacy has emerged as a crucial element in international relations, as nations seek to address the growing threats posed by cyber attacks. The development of international agreements, norms, and principles can promote responsible behavior in cyberspace and can help to reduce the risk of conflict. Bilateral relationships and international organizations can provide a mechanism for nations to work together to address specific cyber threats, while also promoting transparency and mutual understanding. Therefore, the need for cyber diplomacy is likely to grow in importance as the threat of cyber warfare continues to evolve.

FIFTEEN

CYBER WARFARE AND CYBERCRIME

Introduction

Cybercrime and cyber warfare are two of the most significant threats facing governments and organizations worldwide. As technology advances, so does the sophistication and scale of these threats. In this chapter, we will explore the definitions of cybercrime and cyber warfare, their impact on society, and the measures taken to prevent and mitigate them.

What is Cybercrime?

Cybercrime is defined as any illegal activity carried out using the internet or other digital communication technologies. This type of crime includes a wide range of activities such as hacking, phishing, identity theft, and cyberstalking. Cybercriminals often use advanced technologies and techniques to carry out their activities, making them difficult to trace and prosecute.

The Impact of Cybercrime

Cybercrime has a significant impact on individuals, organizations, and governments. It can result in financial loss, reputation damage, and the loss of sensitive information. Cybercriminals can steal personal information such as credit card details and use it to make fraudulent purchases or commit identity theft. They can also target organizations and steal valuable data, trade secrets, and intellectual property. The impact of cybercrime on governments can be devastating, as it can compromise national security and result in the theft of classified information.

Preventing Cybercrime

Preventing cybercrime requires a multifaceted approach that includes education, technology, and policy. Individuals can protect themselves by using strong passwords, avoiding suspicious emails and links, and keeping their software and antivirus programs up to date. Organizations can implement cybersecurity policies, educate their employees, and use advanced technologies such as firewalls and intrusion detection systems. Governments can develop and enforce laws and regulations that criminalize cybercrime and allocate resources to law enforcement agencies to investigate and prosecute cybercriminals.

What is Cyber Warfare?

Cyber warfare is the use of digital technology to carry out attacks on a country's military or civilian infrastructure. Cyber warfare can be carried out by governments, state-sponsored actors, or independent groups. The attacks can range from disrupting communication networks to stealing classified information or even causing physical damage to critical infrastructure such as power plants and water treatment facilities.

The Impact of Cyber Warfare

Cyber warfare has the potential to cause significant damage to a country's infrastructure and economy. It can disrupt essential services such as healthcare, transportation, and communication networks. Cyberattacks on critical infrastructure can result in power outages, water shortages, and other public health and safety risks. In addition, cyber warfare can result in the theft of sensitive information and compromise national security.

Preventing Cyber Warfare

Preventing cyber warfare requires a comprehensive approach that includes diplomacy, international cooperation, and investment in cybersecurity. Governments can work together to develop international treaties and agreements that prohibit cyber warfare and promote cybersecurity. They can also invest in cybersecurity technologies and research to develop advanced defense mechanisms. Organizations can implement cybersecurity measures to protect their infrastructure from cyberattacks and work with law enforcement agencies to report and investigate potential threats.

Conclusion

Cybercrime and cyber warfare are serious threats to individuals, organizations, and governments. Preventing these threats requires a multifaceted approach that includes education, technology, policy, and international cooperation. As technology continues to advance, it is critical that governments, organizations, and individuals remain vigilant in protecting themselves from these threats.

Relationship between Cyber Warfare and Cybercrime

Cyber Warfare and Cybercrime are two closely related and interdependent phenomena that have gained significant importance in recent years. With the increasing reliance on digital technology, the world has become vulnerable to cyber threats, and Cyber Warfare and Cybercrime have become major challenges for governments, organizations, and individuals. While Cyber Warfare refers to the use of digital technology to conduct military operations, Cybercrime refers to the use of digital technology to commit crimes such as identity theft, fraud, and hacking. In this paper, we will explore the relationship between Cyber Warfare and Cybercrime and how they are interconnected.

The Interconnection between Cyber Warfare and Cybercrime:

Cyber Warfare and Cybercrime are interdependent phenomena that are closely related to each other. Cybercrime can be seen as a precursor to Cyber Warfare since many of the techniques and tactics used in Cyber Warfare are borrowed from Cybercrime. Cybercriminals are often the ones who develop and exploit vulnerabilities in software and networks, which are later used by state-sponsored hackers for their military operations. In this sense,

Cybercrime can be seen as a breeding ground for Cyber Warfare.

On the other hand, Cyber Warfare can also lead to Cybercrime. State-sponsored hackers who are involved in Cyber Warfare often steal sensitive information from other countries or organizations, which they can later sell to Cybercriminals. Moreover, Cyber Warfare can also disrupt critical infrastructure, which can create opportunities for Cybercriminals to exploit vulnerabilities in the system.

Furthermore, the line between Cyber Warfare and Cybercrime is becoming increasingly blurred. State-sponsored hackers are often difficult to distinguish from Cybercriminals, as both groups use similar techniques and tactics. State-sponsored hackers may also collaborate with Cybercriminals, as they provide them with the necessary skills and expertise to carry out their operations. Therefore, it is becoming more challenging to differentiate between Cyber Warfare and Cybercrime.

Types of Cyber Warfare and Cybercrime:

There are several types of Cyber Warfare, including espionage, sabotage, and propaganda. Espionage involves the theft of sensitive information from other countries or organizations, while sabotage involves disrupting critical infrastructure such as power grids, communication systems, and financial networks. Propaganda involves the use of digital technology to spread false information and manipulate public opinion.

Similarly, there are several types of Cybercrime, including identity theft, financial fraud, and hacking. Identity theft involves stealing personal information such as social security numbers and credit card numbers, while financial fraud involves using stolen information to make unauthorized purchases or access bank accounts. Hacking involves exploiting vulnerabilities in software and networks to gain unauthorized access to information.

The Relationship between Cyber Warfare and National Security:

Cyber Warfare and Cybercrime have become major challenges for national security. State-sponsored hackers can use Cyber Warfare to disrupt critical infrastructure, steal sensitive information, and manipulate public opinion. This can have serious implications for national security, as it can destabilize governments and economies.

Moreover, Cybercrime can also have serious implications for national security. Cybercriminals can steal sensitive information from governments and organizations, which can compromise national security. They can also use the stolen information to carry out attacks against critical infrastructure, which can have serious implications for national security.

Therefore, governments and organizations are investing significant resources in developing cybersecurity measures to protect against Cyber Warfare and Cybercrime. This includes investing in cybersecurity technologies such as firewalls, intrusion detection systems, and encryption. It also involves developing policies and regulations to deter Cyber Warfare and Cybercrime and to hold those responsible accountable.

Conclusion:

In conclusion, Cyber Warfare and Cybercrime are two closely related and interdependent phenomena that have become major challenges for governments, organizations, and individuals. Cybercrime can be seen as a precursor to Cyber Warfare, and the line between the two is becoming increasingly blurred. State-sponsored hackers often collaborate with Cybercriminals, and it is becoming more challenging to differentiate between the two. Cyber Warfare

Examples of Cybercrime

Cybercrime is a broad term that encompasses a wide range of illegal activities carried out using the internet or other digital communication technologies. Here are some examples of cybercrime:

Hacking: Hacking refers to the unauthorized access to a computer system or network. Hackers can use a variety of techniques such as password cracking, social engineering, and malware to gain access to a system. Once they have access, they can steal data, modify or delete files, and cause other forms of damage.

Malware: Malware refers to any software that is designed to harm a computer system or network. Examples of malware include viruses, Trojans, and ransomware. Malware can be used to steal data, encrypt files, and cause other forms of damage.

Phishing: Phishing is a type of social engineering attack that involves sending fraudulent emails or messages to individuals in an attempt to trick them into revealing sensitive information such as passwords or credit card details. Phishing emails may appear to come from legitimate sources, such as a bank or social media platform.

Identity Theft: Identity theft refers to the theft of personal information such as social security numbers, credit card details, and passwords. Cybercriminals can use this information to make fraudulent purchases or commit other types of fraud.

Cyberbullying: Cyberbullying involves the use of digital technologies to harass, intimidate, or threaten individuals. Cyberbullying can take many forms, such as sending threatening messages or posting offensive content on social media.

Online Scams: Online scams are schemes that are designed to trick individuals into sending money or providing sensitive information. Examples of online scams include lottery scams, investment scams, and romance scams.

DDoS Attacks: A DDoS (Distributed Denial of Service) attack is a type of cyber attack that involves flooding a website or network with traffic to the point where it becomes unavailable. DDoS attacks can be carried out using botnets or other means.

Cyber Espionage: Cyber espionage refers to the use of digital technologies to gather sensitive information from other countries, organizations, or individuals. Cyber espionage can be carried out by governments or state-sponsored actors.

Cyberstalking: Cyberstalking involves the use of digital technologies to harass, intimidate, or stalk individuals.

Cyberstalkers may use social media, email, or other means to contact their victims.

Conclusion

Cybercrime is a significant threat to individuals, organizations, and governments. As technology continues to advance, so do the techniques and scale of cybercrime. It is essential to remain vigilant and take steps to protect yourself from cybercrime, such as using strong passwords, keeping your software up to date, and being cautious about clicking on suspicious links or emails. Organizations can also implement cybersecurity measures, such as firewalls and intrusion detection systems, to protect their infrastructure from cyber attacks.

The need for Cybercrime legislation

With the increasing reliance on digital technology, Cybercrime has become a major threat to individuals, organizations, and governments. Cybercriminals use digital technology to commit crimes such as identity theft, fraud, and hacking, which can have serious implications for individuals and organizations. Therefore, there is a need for Cybercrime legislation to deter Cybercrime and to hold those responsible accountable. In this paper, we will discuss the need for Cybercrime legislation and how it can help to combat Cybercrime.

The Need for Cybercrime Legislation:

Cybercrime legislation is necessary for several reasons. Firstly, Cybercrime is a global problem, and legislation can help to harmonize laws across different jurisdictions. Cybercriminals can operate from anywhere in the world, and it can be difficult to bring them to justice without international cooperation. Cybercrime legislation can help to facilitate international cooperation and make it easier to prosecute Cybercriminals.

Secondly, Cybercrime legislation can help to define Cybercrime and make it easier to identify and prosecute Cybercriminals. Cybercrime is a complex and evolving phenomenon, and legislation can help to keep pace with new forms of Cybercrime. Legislation can help to define Cybercrime and provide clear guidelines on what constitutes a Cybercrime. This can help law enforcement agencies to identify Cybercrime and take appropriate action.

Thirdly, Cybercrime legislation can help to deter Cybercrime by providing harsher punishments for Cybercriminals. Cybercrime can have serious implications for individuals and organizations, and the punishments for Cybercrime should reflect this. Cybercrime legislation can help to provide clear guidelines on the punishments for different types of Cybercrime and make it clear that Cybercrime will not be tolerated.

Fourthly, Cybercrime legislation can help to protect individuals and organizations from Cybercrime. Cybercrime legislation can help to establish measures to prevent Cybercrime, such as requiring organizations to implement cybersecurity measures and providing individuals with guidance on how to protect themselves from Cybercrime. Legislation can also help to establish measures to assist victims of Cybercrime, such as providing them with access to legal remedies and compensation.

Finally, Cybercrime legislation can help to promote trust in digital technology. As the world becomes increasingly reliant on digital technology, trust in digital technology is becoming increasingly important. Cybercrime can undermine trust in digital technology, and legislation can help to reassure individuals and organizations that the use of digital technology is safe and secure.

Conclusion:

In conclusion, Cybercrime is a major threat to individuals, organizations, and governments, and Cybercrime legislation is necessary to combat Cybercrime. Cybercrime legislation can help to harmonize laws across different jurisdictions, define Cybercrime, deter Cybercrime, protect individuals and organizations from Cybercrime, and promote trust in digital technology. Therefore, governments and organizations should invest in Cybercrime legislation to ensure that Cybercrime is dealt with effectively and that individuals and organizations can use digital technology safely and securely.

Defining Cyber Warfare and Cybercrime

Cyber warfare is the use of digital technologies to conduct military operations or attacks against another country or entity. This can include hacking into computer networks to steal or destroy sensitive information, disrupting communication systems, or causing physical damage to infrastructure. Cyber warfare can be carried out by both state and non-state actors.

Cybercrime, on the other hand, refers to any illegal activity that is carried out using digital technologies. Cybercrime can take many forms, including hacking, identity theft, online scams, and cyberbullying. Cybercriminals can target individuals, organizations, and even governments.

Examples of Cyber Warfare

Stuxnet Worm: The Stuxnet worm is a computer virus that was discovered in 2010. It is believed to have been developed by the US and Israel as a means of disrupting Iran's nuclear program. The virus was designed to attack industrial control systems, specifically those used in nuclear facilities, and cause physical damage.

Russian Cyber Attacks: Russia has been accused of carrying out cyber attacks against several countries, including the US and Ukraine. These attacks have included hacking into government and military systems, stealing sensitive information, and disrupting critical infrastructure.

Chinese Cyber Espionage: China has been accused of engaging in cyber espionage against other countries and corporations. This includes stealing sensitive information from government and military systems, as well as from private companies.

North Korean Cyber Attacks: North Korea has been accused of carrying out several cyber attacks against other countries and entities. These attacks have included hacking into government and military systems, stealing sensitive information, and disrupting critical infrastructure.

Examples of Cybercrime

WannaCry Ransomware Attack: The WannaCry ransomware attack was a global cyber attack that occurred in 2017. The attack targeted computers running Microsoft Windows and encrypted the files on the infected computers. The attackers demanded a ransom in exchange for the decryption key.

Yahoo Data Breach: In 2013 and 2014, Yahoo experienced two data breaches that compromised the personal information of millions of users. The attackers were able to steal names, email addresses, dates of birth, and other sensitive information.

Target Data Breach: In 2013, Target experienced a data breach that compromised the credit and debit card information of millions of customers. The attackers were able to gain access to the data by stealing login credentials from a third-party vendor.

Ashley Madison Data Breach: In 2015, the Ashley Madison dating website was hacked, and the personal information of millions of users was stolen. The attackers threatened to release the information unless the site was shut down.

Preventing and Responding to Cyber Warfare and Cybercrime

Preventing cyber warfare and cybercrime requires a multifaceted approach that involves both individuals and organizations. Here are some measures that can be taken to prevent and respond to these types of attacks:

Education: Educating individuals and organizations about the risks of cyber attacks and the measures that can be taken to prevent them is critical. This can include training employees on how to spot phishing emails, using strong passwords, and keeping software up to date.

Cybersecurity Measures: Implementing cybersecurity measures such as firewalls, intrusion detection systems, and encryption can help protect against cyber attacks.

International Cooperation: Cyber warfare and cybercrime

Examples of Cybercrime

With the increasing reliance on digital technology, Cybercrime has become a major threat to individuals, organizations, and governments. Cybercriminals use digital technology to commit crimes such as identity theft, fraud, and hacking, which can have serious implications for individuals and organizations. In this paper, we will discuss examples of Cybercrime and their impact.

Examples of Cybercrime:

Identity Theft:

Identity theft is one of the most common types of Cybercrime. It involves stealing personal information, such as name, date of birth, social security number, and financial information, and using it for fraudulent purposes. Cybercriminals can obtain personal information through phishing scams, hacking, or malware. The impact of identity theft can be severe, as victims may suffer financial loss and damage to their credit score.

Phishing:

Phishing is a type of Cybercrime that involves tricking individuals into giving away their personal information, such as usernames and passwords, by pretending to be a trustworthy entity, such as a bank or a social media platform. Phishing scams can be carried out through emails, text messages, or phone calls. The impact of phishing can be significant, as victims may have their personal information stolen and used for fraudulent purposes.

Ransomware:

Ransomware is a type of malware that encrypts a victim's files and demands payment in exchange for the decryption key. Cybercriminals can use phishing scams, social engineering, or vulnerabilities in software to infect a victim's device with ransomware. The impact of ransomware can be severe, as victims may lose access to their files and suffer financial loss if they choose to pay the ransom.

Hacking:

Hacking is a type of Cybercrime that involves gaining unauthorized access to a computer system or network.

Cybercriminals can use hacking to steal sensitive information, disrupt services, or carry out further attacks. The impact of hacking can be significant, as victims may suffer financial loss, damage to their reputation, or legal consequences.

Cyberbullying:

Cyberbullying is a type of Cybercrime that involves using digital technology to harass, intimidate, or threaten an individual. Cyberbullies can use social media, messaging apps, or online forums to carry out their attacks. The impact of cyberbullying can be severe, as victims may suffer from emotional distress, depression, or even suicide.

Child Sexual Exploitation:

Child sexual exploitation is a type of Cybercrime that involves the sexual abuse or exploitation of children through digital technology. Cybercriminals can use the internet to groom children, share indecent images, or engage in sexual activity. The impact of child sexual exploitation can be devastating, as victims may suffer from long-term psychological harm and struggle to form healthy relationships.

Conclusion:

In conclusion, Cybercrime is a major threat to individuals, organizations, and governments, and examples of Cybercrime include identity theft, phishing, ransomware, hacking, cyberbullying, and child sexual exploitation. The impact of Cybercrime can be severe, and it is important for individuals and organizations to take measures to protect themselves from Cybercrime, such as implementing strong cybersecurity measures and being vigilant against suspicious emails and messages. Governments also need to invest in Cybercrime legislation and law enforcement agencies to ensure that Cybercrime is dealt with effectively and that victims are provided with the support they need.

SIXTEEN

Emerging Technologies in Cyber Warfare

Introduction

As technology continues to advance, so do the tools and methods used in cyber warfare. New technologies such as artificial intelligence, blockchain, and the Internet of Things (IoT) are changing the landscape of cyber warfare, and it is important for governments, militaries, and organizations to stay informed about these emerging technologies and the potential threats they pose. In this chapter, we will explore some of the emerging technologies in cyber warfare, their potential uses, and the potential risks they pose.

Artificial Intelligence (AI) in Cyber Warfare

Artificial intelligence has the potential to revolutionize cyber warfare in several ways. One of the most significant ways AI is being used in cyber warfare is in the development of autonomous cyber weapons. These weapons would be able to identify vulnerabilities in target systems and launch attacks without human intervention.

Another potential use for AI in cyber warfare is in the development of AI-powered defensive measures. These measures could be used to detect and prevent cyber attacks in real-time, as well as to respond to attacks more effectively.

However, the use of AI in cyber warfare also poses significant risks. For example, autonomous cyber weapons could be difficult to control and could potentially cause unintended damage. Additionally, the use of AI in cyber warfare could lead to a new arms race, as countries and organizations compete to develop the most advanced AI-powered weapons.

Blockchain in Cyber Warfare

Blockchain technology, which is best known for its use in cryptocurrency transactions, also has potential uses in cyber warfare. One potential application is in secure communication and data storage. Blockchain technology can be used to create a secure, decentralized network that is resistant to tampering and hacking.

Another potential use for blockchain in cyber warfare is in the development of secure supply chain management. By using blockchain to track and verify the authenticity of components and software, organizations can ensure that their systems are not compromised by malicious actors.

However, the use of blockchain in cyber warfare also poses risks. For example, the decentralized nature of blockchain makes it difficult to regulate, which could lead to the development of black markets for cyber weapons and other malicious tools.

Internet of Things (IoT) in Cyber Warfare

The Internet of Things (IoT) refers to the network of devices and appliances that are connected to the internet, such as smart home devices, wearables, and industrial control systems. As the number of connected devices continues to grow, so does the potential attack surface for cyber criminals.

One potential use for IoT in cyber warfare is in the development of botnets. Botnets are networks of compromised devices that can be used to launch coordinated attacks on target systems. With the widespread adoption of IoT devices, botnets could become even more powerful and difficult to detect.

Another potential risk of IoT in cyber warfare is the vulnerability of industrial control systems. These systems are used to control critical infrastructure, such as power grids and water treatment plants. If these systems are compromised, it could have devastating consequences.

Preventing and Responding to Emerging Technologies in Cyber Warfare

As new technologies continue to emerge, it is important for governments, militaries, and organizations to stay informed about the potential risks and to take steps to mitigate them. Here are some measures that can be taken to prevent and respond to emerging technologies in cyber warfare:

Research and Development: Investing in research and development can help governments and organizations stay ahead of the curve in terms of emerging technologies in cyber warfare. By developing new defensive measures and countermeasures, it may be possible to mitigate the risks posed by these technologies.

Education and Training: Educating individuals and organizations about the potential risks of emerging technologies in cyber warfare is critical. This can include training employees on how to spot and prevent cyber attacks, as well as on the risks posed by emerging technologies.

Collaboration and Information Sharing: Collaboration and information sharing between governments and organizations

As technology continues to advance, so do the tools and methods used in cyber warfare. New technologies such as artificial intelligence, blockchain, and the Internet of Things (IoT) are changing the landscape of cyber warfare, and it is important for governments, militaries, and organizations to stay informed about these emerging technologies and the potential threats they pose. In this chapter, we will explore some of the emerging technologies in cyber warfare, their potential uses, and the potential risks they pose.

Artificial Intelligence (AI) in Cyber Warfare

Artificial intelligence has the potential to revolutionize cyber warfare in several ways. One of the most significant ways AI is being used in cyber warfare is in the development of autonomous cyber weapons. These weapons would be able to identify vulnerabilities in target systems and launch attacks without human intervention.

Another potential use for AI in cyber warfare is in the development of AI-powered defensive measures. These measures could be used to detect and prevent cyber attacks in real-time, as well as to respond to attacks more effectively.

However, the use of AI in cyber warfare also poses significant risks. For example, autonomous cyber weapons could be difficult to control and could potentially cause unintended damage. Additionally, the use of AI in cyber warfare could lead to a new arms race, as countries and organizations compete to develop the most advanced AI-powered weapons.

One example of how AI is being used in cyber warfare is the development of the Stuxnet worm, which was used to target Iran's nuclear program in 2010. The worm was able to identify and exploit vulnerabilities in industrial control systems, causing physical damage to centrifuges used in the nuclear program. The use of AI in the development of such sophisticated cyber weapons is likely to become more common in the future.

Blockchain in Cyber Warfare

Blockchain technology, which is best known for its use in cryptocurrency transactions, also has potential uses in cyber warfare. One potential application is in secure communication and data storage. Blockchain technology can be used to create a secure, decentralized network that is resistant to tampering and hacking.

Another potential use for blockchain in cyber warfare is in the development of secure supply chain management. By using blockchain to track and verify the authenticity of components and software, organizations can ensure that their systems are not compromised by malicious actors.

However, the use of blockchain in cyber warfare also poses risks. For example, the decentralized nature of blockchain makes it difficult to regulate, which could lead to the development of black markets for cyber weapons and other malicious tools.

One example of how blockchain is being used in cyber warfare is the development of the U.S. Department of Defense's (DoD) Cybersecurity Capability Maturity Model (C2M2) program. This program uses blockchain to provide a secure, decentralized method of tracking and assessing the cybersecurity readiness of DoD contractors.

Internet of Things (IoT) in Cyber Warfare

The Internet of Things (IoT) refers to the network of devices and appliances that are connected to the internet, such as smart home devices, wearables, and industrial control systems. As the number of connected devices continues to grow, so does the potential attack surface for cyber criminals.

One potential use for IoT in cyber warfare is in the development of botnets. Botnets are networks of compromised devices that can be used to launch coordinated attacks on target systems. With the widespread adoption of IoT devices, botnets could become even more powerful and difficult to detect.

Another potential risk of IoT in cyber warfare is the vulnerability of industrial control systems. These systems are used to control critical infrastructure, such as power grids and water treatment plants. If these systems are compromised, it could have devastating consequences.

One example of how IoT is being used in cyber warfare is the Mirai botnet, which was used to launch a DDoS attack on DNS provider Dyn in 2016

SEVENTEEN

THE FUTURE OF CYBER WARFARE

The future of cyber warfare is a complex and evolving landscape that poses significant challenges to governments, militaries, and civilians around the world. As technology continues to advance and become increasingly integrated into all aspects of our lives, the potential for cyber attacks and their consequences becomes more significant.

One of the most significant trends in cyber warfare is the increasing sophistication of attacks. Hackers and state-sponsored actors are constantly developing new techniques and technologies to penetrate networks, steal data, and cause damage. For example, in recent years, we have seen the emergence of advanced persistent threats (APTs), which are sophisticated and highly targeted attacks that are difficult to detect and mitigate.

Another trend is the growing use of artificial intelligence (AI) and machine learning (ML) in cyber attacks. These technologies can be used to automate the process of identifying vulnerabilities in a target's network and exploiting them, as well as to evade detection by security systems. In addition, AI and ML can be used to develop more effective and targeted social engineering attacks, such as spear phishing.

One potential outcome of these trends is the increased likelihood of large-scale cyber attacks that could disrupt critical infrastructure or cause widespread economic damage. For example, a successful attack on a power grid or financial system could have devastating consequences for a country's economy and national security. As such, many governments and militaries are investing heavily in cybersecurity to prevent such attacks and to develop effective response plans in case they do occur.

Another potential outcome is the blurring of the line between cyber warfare and traditional warfare. As militaries increasingly rely on networked technology to carry out their missions, they become more vulnerable to cyber attacks. At the same time, they are also developing their own cyber capabilities, which could be used in conjunction with more traditional military tactics. This could lead to a situation where cyber attacks are used as a prelude to, or in conjunction with, traditional military operations.

The rise of cyber espionage is also a major concern for governments around the world. State-sponsored actors are constantly seeking to gain access to sensitive information that can be used to gain a strategic advantage. This information can range from military secrets to trade secrets and intellectual property. In some cases, cyber espionage can also be used to disrupt political processes or to influence public opinion.

In addition to state-sponsored actors, there is also a growing threat from non-state actors such as hacktivists and cyber criminals. These groups can carry out attacks for a variety of reasons, including political activism, financial gain, or simply for the challenge. As such, they can be difficult to predict and even more challenging to defend against.

Overall, the future of cyber warfare is complex and uncertain. While technological advances offer new opportunities for attackers, they also provide new tools for defenders. As such, it is essential that governments, militaries, and civilians continue to invest in cybersecurity and work together to develop effective strategies for preventing and responding to cyber attacks. By doing so, we can help to ensure that the benefits of technology continue to be realized while minimizing the risks.

The future of cyber warfare is a complex and rapidly evolving landscape that presents significant challenges to governments, militaries, and civilians around the world. As technology continues to advance and become increasingly integrated into all aspects of our lives, the potential for cyber attacks and their consequences becomes more significant. This chapter will explore the future of cyber warfare and its potential impact on global security.

One of the most significant trends in cyber warfare is the increasing sophistication of attacks. Hackers and state-sponsored actors are constantly developing new techniques and technologies to penetrate networks, steal data, and cause damage. For example, in recent years, we have seen the emergence of advanced persistent threats (APTs), which are sophisticated and highly targeted attacks that are difficult to detect and mitigate.

APTs are often designed to remain undetected for extended periods of time, allowing the attacker to gather as much data as possible before being discovered. These attacks are typically launched against high-value targets such as government agencies, military organizations, and large corporations. APTs can be used to steal sensitive data, such as intellectual property, trade secrets, and government secrets, or to disrupt critical infrastructure such as power grids, transportation systems, and financial institutions.

Another trend in cyber warfare is the growing use of artificial intelligence (AI) and machine learning (ML). These technologies can be used to automate the process of identifying vulnerabilities in a target's network and exploiting them, as well as to evade detection by security systems. In addition, AI and ML can be used to develop more effective and targeted social engineering attacks, such as spear phishing.

One potential outcome of these trends is the increased likelihood of large-scale cyber attacks that could disrupt critical infrastructure or cause widespread economic damage. For example, a successful attack on a power grid or financial system could have devastating consequences for a country's economy and national security. As such, many governments and militaries are investing heavily in cybersecurity to prevent such attacks and to develop effective response plans in case they do occur.

Another potential outcome is the blurring of the line between cyber warfare and traditional warfare. As militaries increasingly rely on networked technology to carry out their missions, they become more vulnerable to cyber attacks. At the same time, they are also developing their own cyber capabilities, which could be used in conjunction with more traditional military tactics. This could lead to a situation where cyber attacks are used as a prelude to, or in conjunction with, traditional military operations.

One example of this is the Stuxnet worm, which was a computer virus that was used to attack Iran's nuclear program in 2010. The virus was designed to specifically target and destroy centrifuges used to enrich uranium. The attack was a joint operation between the United States and Israel and is considered to be the first known example of a cyber weapon being used in conjunction with traditional military tactics.

The rise of cyber espionage is also a major concern for governments around the world. State-sponsored actors are constantly seeking to gain access to sensitive information that can be used to gain a strategic advantage. This information can range from military secrets to trade secrets and intellectual property. In some cases, cyber espionage can also be used to disrupt political processes or to influence public opinion.

One recent example of cyber espionage is the SolarWinds attack, which was discovered in December 2020. The attack involved hackers gaining access to SolarWinds' software and using it to distribute a Trojan horse malware called SUNBURST to the company's customers. The malware allowed the hackers to gain access to sensitive data, including emails, intellectual property, and government secrets.

In addition to state-sponsored actors, there is also a growing threat from non-state actors such as hacktivists and cyber criminals. These groups can carry out attacks for a variety of reasons, including political activism, financial gain, or simply for the challenge.

EIGHTEEN

CYBER WARFARE AND THE PUBLIC

As cyber warfare continues to evolve, it is becoming increasingly important for the public to be aware of the potential risks and to take steps to protect themselves. In this chapter, we will explore the role of the public in cyber warfare, including the potential risks they face, the importance of cybersecurity education, and ways in which individuals can protect themselves.

The Risks of Cyber Warfare for the Public

Cyber warfare poses several risks to the general public, including:

Personal data theft: Cyber criminals can steal personal data, such as credit card information and Social Security numbers, to commit identity theft or financial fraud.

Ransomware attacks: Ransomware is a type of malware that encrypts a user's files and demands payment in exchange for the decryption key.

Phishing attacks: Phishing is a type of social engineering attack in which cyber criminals use deceptive tactics to trick individuals into divulging sensitive information.

Distributed denial of service (DDoS) attacks: DDoS attacks are designed to overwhelm a target system with traffic, causing it to crash or become unavailable.

Malware infections: Malware can infect a user's computer and steal personal information, or use the computer to launch attacks on other systems.

Cyberbullying: Cyberbullying is a type of online harassment that can have serious consequences for victims.

Cybersecurity Education for the Public

Given the potential risks of cyber warfare, it is important for the public to be educated about cybersecurity. This education can take many forms, including:

Training programs: Governments and organizations can offer training programs that teach individuals about the risks of cyber warfare and how to protect themselves.

Public awareness campaigns: Public awareness campaigns can help raise awareness about the risks of cyber warfare and the importance of cybersecurity.

School curricula: Schools can incorporate cybersecurity education into their curricula to ensure that students are aware of the risks and how to protect themselves.

Workshops and seminars: Workshops and seminars can be held to teach individuals about cybersecurity best practices and how to avoid common pitfalls.

Protecting Yourself from Cyber Warfare

There are several steps that individuals can take to protect themselves from cyber warfare:

Keep software up to date: Keeping software up to date is one of the most important things individuals can do to protect themselves from cyber attacks.

Use strong passwords: Strong passwords can help prevent unauthorized access to accounts.

Be cautious of suspicious emails and messages: Phishing attacks often rely on convincing individuals to divulge sensitive information, so it is important to be cautious of suspicious emails and messages.

Use antivirus software: Antivirus software can help detect and remove malware infections.

Back up important data: Backing up important data can help mitigate the damage caused by ransomware attacks.

Be cautious of public Wi-Fi: Public Wi-Fi networks can be insecure, so it is important to be cautious when using them.

Conclusion

As cyber warfare continues to evolve, it is becoming increasingly important for the public to be aware of the potential risks and to take steps to protect themselves. By educating individuals about cybersecurity best practices and taking steps to protect personal information, we can help reduce the impact of cyber warfare on the general public.

NINETEEN
Cyber Warfare and Education

As technology continues to advance and become increasingly integrated into all aspects of our lives, the need for cybersecurity education becomes more pressing. Cyber attacks can have significant consequences, including financial loss, identity theft, and national security threats. As such, it is essential that individuals, businesses, and governments are educated about cybersecurity best practices and how to protect themselves against cyber attacks. This chapter will explore the importance of cybersecurity education and its impact on cyber warfare.

The Need for Cybersecurity Education

Cybersecurity education is essential in today's digital age. The internet has become an integral part of our daily lives, and we rely on it for communication, shopping, banking, and more. However, the more we use technology, the more vulnerable we become to cyber attacks. As such, it is essential that we understand the risks and take steps to protect ourselves.

Cybersecurity education is not just important for individuals. Businesses and governments also need to be educated about cybersecurity risks and how to protect their networks and data. Cyber attacks can have significant consequences for businesses, including financial loss and damage to reputation. Governments also need to be aware of cybersecurity risks, as cyber attacks can pose a significant threat to national security.

The Impact of Cybersecurity Education on Cyber Warfare

Cybersecurity education can have a significant impact on cyber warfare. A well-educated population is less likely to fall victim to cyber attacks, which can help to reduce the effectiveness of cyber warfare. Additionally, cybersecurity education can help businesses and governments to better protect their networks and data, making it more difficult for cyber attackers to penetrate their systems.

One of the challenges of cyber warfare is that attackers can come from anywhere in the world. As such, it is essential that cybersecurity education is accessible to people in all parts of the world. Governments and non-governmental organizations (NGOs) can play an important role in providing cybersecurity education to people in developing countries, where the risk of cyber attacks may be higher due to lower levels of security and education.

The Role of Schools and Universities in Cybersecurity Education

Schools and universities can play an important role in cybersecurity education. They can provide students with the skills and knowledge they need to protect themselves against cyber attacks and to pursue careers in cybersecurity. In addition, schools and universities can work with businesses and governments to develop cybersecurity programs that are tailored to their specific needs.

Many schools and universities are already offering cybersecurity courses and programs. For example, the National Cyber Security Centre in the UK offers a range of cybersecurity courses and programs for schools and universities. In the US, the National Science Foundation has established the CyberCorps Scholarship for Service program, which provides funding for students pursuing cybersecurity degrees in exchange for a commitment to work for the government after graduation.

However, there is still much work to be done in terms of cybersecurity education. According to a survey by the Ponemon Institute, only 35% of IT professionals believe that their organizations provide adequate cybersecurity training. This highlights the need for greater investment in cybersecurity education and training.

Best Practices for Cybersecurity Education

There are several best practices that can be used to improve cybersecurity education. These include:

Tailoring education to the audience: Cybersecurity education should be tailored to the needs of the audience. For example, cybersecurity education for children should focus on online safety and responsible internet use, while cybersecurity education for businesses should focus on protecting networks and data.

Keeping education up to date: Cybersecurity threats are constantly evolving, and cybersecurity education needs to keep up. Education should be regularly updated to reflect the latest threats and best practices.

Providing hands-on experience: Cybersecurity education should provide hands-on experience to help students develop practical skills. This could include simulated cyber attacks or practical exercises in protecting networks and data.

Fostering collaboration: Cybersecurity education should foster collaboration between different groups,

including businesses, governments, and NGOs. Collaboration can help to improve cybersecurity education and develop new solutions to cybersecurity threats.

Emphasizing the importance of cybersecurity culture: Cybersecurity education should emphasize the importance of creating a culture of cybersecurity. This means that cybersecurity should be a priority for everyone, not just IT professionals. Creating a culture of cybersecurity can help to reduce the risk of cyber attacks and improve overall cybersecurity.

Challenges in Cybersecurity Education

Despite the importance of cybersecurity education, there are several challenges that need to be addressed. One of the biggest challenges is the lack of qualified cybersecurity professionals. The demand for cybersecurity professionals is growing rapidly, but there is a shortage of skilled workers to fill these positions. This is a significant challenge for businesses and governments, as they struggle to find the talent they need to protect their networks and data.

Another challenge is the rapidly evolving nature of cybersecurity threats. Cyber attacks are becoming more sophisticated, and cybersecurity education needs to keep up. This requires regular updates to cybersecurity education programs and the development of new solutions to cybersecurity threats.

The cost of cybersecurity education can also be a significant barrier. Many cybersecurity education programs are expensive, which can make them inaccessible to some individuals and organizations. This is a particular challenge for small businesses and developing countries, which may not have the resources to invest in cybersecurity education.

Finally, there is a lack of awareness about the importance of cybersecurity education. Many individuals and organizations do not understand the risks of cyber attacks and the need for cybersecurity education. This highlights the importance of raising awareness about cybersecurity and its impact on individuals, businesses, and governments.

Conclusion

In conclusion, cybersecurity education is essential in today's digital age. Cyber attacks can have significant consequences, including financial loss, identity theft, and national security threats. As such, it is essential that individuals, businesses, and governments are educated about cybersecurity risks and how to protect themselves against cyber attacks.

Schools and universities can play an important role in cybersecurity education, providing students with the skills and knowledge they need to pursue careers in cybersecurity and to protect themselves against cyber attacks. However, there are several challenges that need to be addressed, including the shortage of qualified cybersecurity professionals, the rapidly evolving nature of cybersecurity threats, the cost of cybersecurity education, and the lack of awareness about the importance of cybersecurity education.

By addressing these challenges and investing in cybersecurity education, we can improve our ability to protect ourselves against cyber attacks and reduce the effectiveness of cyber warfare. Cybersecurity education is an essential tool in the fight against cyber attacks, and we must continue to prioritize it in order to ensure our safety and security in the digital age.

In conclusion, the future of cyber warfare is complex and constantly evolving, with new technologies and tactics emerging all the time. It is clear that cyber warfare poses a significant threat to individuals, businesses, and governments, and that the consequences of cyber attacks can be severe.

To address these challenges, it is essential that we continue to invest in cybersecurity research and development, as well as in cybersecurity education. By staying informed about the latest cybersecurity threats and developments, we can better protect ourselves and our organizations against cyber attacks.

We must also continue to collaborate across different sectors and industries, sharing information and best practices in order to improve cybersecurity. By creating a culture of cybersecurity and emphasizing its importance to all individuals and organizations, we can reduce the risk of cyber attacks and improve our overall cybersecurity posture.

In short, the future of cyber warfare is uncertain, but by working together and prioritizing cybersecurity, we can better protect ourselves against this evolving threat. We must remain vigilant and continue to adapt to new threats and challenges as they arise, in order to ensure our safety and security in the digital age.

TWENTY

CONCLUSION, SUMMARY & FUTURE

In this book, we have examined the complex and rapidly evolving landscape of cyber warfare. From the early days of computer viruses and hacking, to the sophisticated and highly targeted attacks of today, we have seen how the tools and tactics of cyber warfare have become increasingly advanced.

Summary of Cyber Warfare:

Throughout this book, we have explored a range of topics related to cyber warfare, including:

The history of cyber warfare: We have examined the origins of cyber warfare, including the first documented cases of computer viruses and other forms of digital attack.

The tools and tactics of cyber warfare: We have looked at the various tools and tactics that are used in cyber warfare, including malware, phishing, and distributed denial-of-service (DDoS) attacks.

The actors involved in cyber warfare: We have explored the various actors involved in cyber warfare, including nation-states, cybercriminals, and hacktivists.

The impact of cyber warfare: We have seen how cyber warfare can have a significant impact on individuals, organizations, and even entire countries.

Future implications of Cyber Warfare:

Looking to the future, it is clear that cyber warfare will continue to be a significant threat. As technology continues to evolve, so too will the tools and tactics used in cyber warfare. We can expect to see more sophisticated attacks, targeting not just individuals and organizations, but also critical infrastructure and even entire nations.

One potential future scenario is a large-scale cyber attack that targets critical infrastructure such as power grids or transportation systems. Such an attack could have devastating consequences, causing widespread disruption and potentially even loss of life.

Another future trend to watch is the increasing use of artificial intelligence (AI) in cyber warfare. As AI becomes more advanced, it is likely that cyber attackers will use it to develop more effective and targeted attacks.

Final thoughts and recommendations:

In light of the ongoing threat of cyber warfare, it is essential that individuals and organizations take steps to protect themselves. Some key recommendations include:

Use strong passwords and multi-factor authentication: One of the simplest yet most effective ways to protect against cyber attacks is to use strong, unique passwords and enable multi-factor authentication wherever possible.

Keep software up to date: Software vulnerabilities are a common entry point for cyber attackers. By keeping software up to date, you can ensure that any known vulnerabilities are patched.

Be cautious of suspicious emails and links: Phishing attacks remain a common tactic used by cybercriminals. Be wary of any unsolicited emails or links, and always verify the source before clicking.

Implement cybersecurity training: Training employees on basic cybersecurity best practices can go a long way in preventing cyber attacks.

Invest in cybersecurity solutions: Finally, organizations should invest in cybersecurity solutions such as firewalls, antivirus software, and intrusion detection systems to help protect against cyber attacks.

Summarize the key themes and insights from your book: Provide a brief overview of the topics covered in your book, highlighting the main themes and insights that emerged. This will help readers understand the key takeaways and conclusions.

Discuss the implications of your findings: Consider the implications of your research for the broader field of cybersecurity and cyber warfare. Are there any new threats or trends that emerged during your research? What are the potential consequences of these threats or trends?

Make recommendations for future research or action: Based on your research, what are the areas that require further investigation or intervention? What steps can individuals or organizations take to protect themselves against cyber attacks? Are there any policy or regulatory changes that are needed to improve cybersecurity?

Provide a concluding statement: End the chapter with a concluding statement that summarizes the main points of the chapter and reinforces the significance of your research. This statement should leave readers with a sense of closure and understanding of the importance of your work.

It's important to remember that the length of the conclusion chapter may vary depending on the overall length of your book and the amount of content covered in the preceding chapters. However, aim to provide enough detail and insight to make it a comprehensive and satisfying conclusion to your book.

In conclusion, cyber warfare is a complex and rapidly evolving threat. As we move into the future, it is essential that individuals and organizations remain vigilant and take steps to protect themselves against cyber attacks. By doing so, we can help ensure a more secure and resilient digital world.

---*End The Book*--

9 798889 866480

Printed by Libri Plureos GmbH in Hamburg, Germany